The Old Courthouse

Americans Build a Forum on the Frontier

Donald F. Dosch

Editor: Dan Murphy
Design Consultant: Michelle Taverniti

Contents

Next page: *The Old
Courthouse and downtown St.
Louis: view from top of
Gateway Arch.*
Page 4-5: *The Old Courthouse
from the east sidewalk.*
Photos by Joseph Matthews:
Courtesy Jefferson National
Expansion Memorial

Prologue

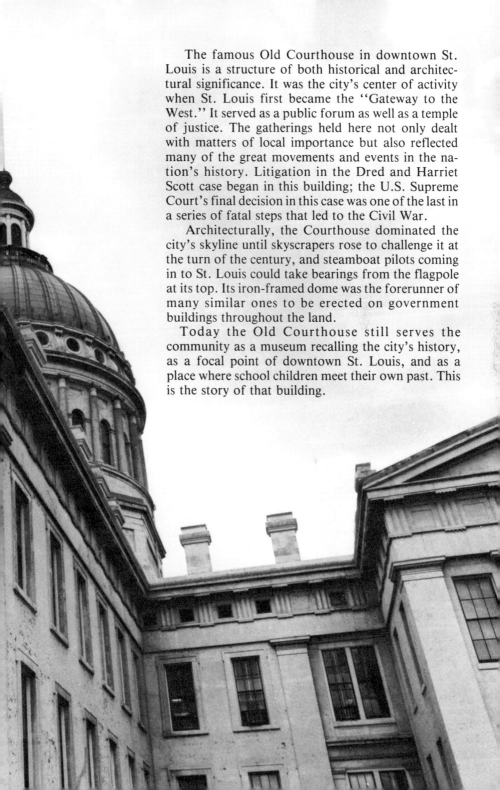

The famous Old Courthouse in downtown St. Louis is a structure of both historical and architectural significance. It was the city's center of activity when St. Louis first became the "Gateway to the West." It served as a public forum as well as a temple of justice. The gatherings held here not only dealt with matters of local importance but also reflected many of the great movements and events in the nation's history. Litigation in the Dred and Harriet Scott case began in this building; the U.S. Supreme Court's final decision in this case was one of the last in a series of fatal steps that led to the Civil War.

Architecturally, the Courthouse dominated the city's skyline until skyscrapers rose to challenge it at the turn of the century, and steamboat pilots coming in to St. Louis could take bearings from the flagpole at its top. Its iron-framed dome was the forerunner of many similar ones to be erected on government buildings throughout the land.

Today the Old Courthouse still serves the community as a museum recalling the city's history, as a focal point of downtown St. Louis, and as a place where school children meet their own past. This is the story of that building.

The wrought and cast iron dome of the Old Courthouse was one of the first of its kind. In the "cupola," or "lantern," leaded glass windows allow light into the very top, while keeping out the weather. The dome actually is two layers, with room between for bracing and working access. Courtesy Jefferson National Expansion Memorial

7

Details: *Cornice and exterior columns.* Courtesy Jefferson National Expansion Memorial

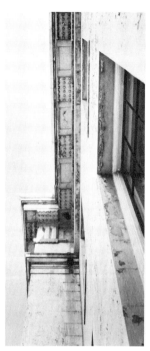

Details: *Yard, fence and furnishings.* Courtesy Jefferson National Expansion Memorial

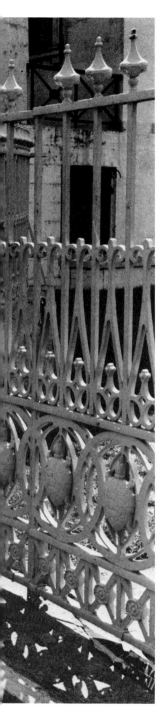

Details: *Porches, doors, and windows.* Courtesy Jefferson National Expansion Memorial

Reflection from the Equitable Building, neighbor of the Old Courthouse on the south side. Courtesy Jefferson National Expansion Memorial

14

The Building

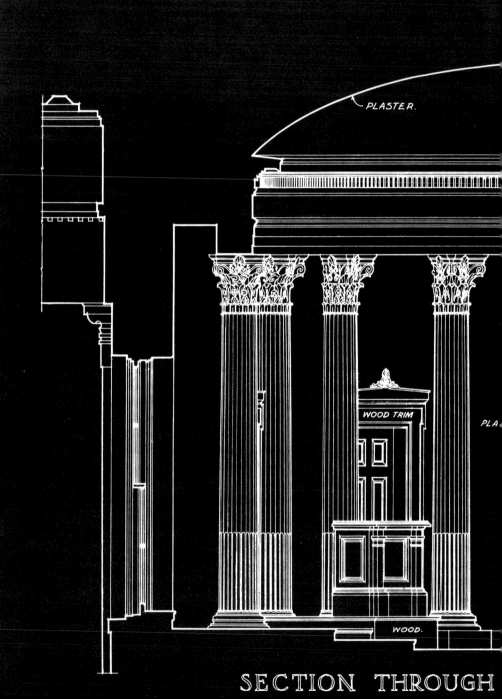

PLASTER.

WOOD TRIM

PLA

WOOD.

SECTION THROUGH

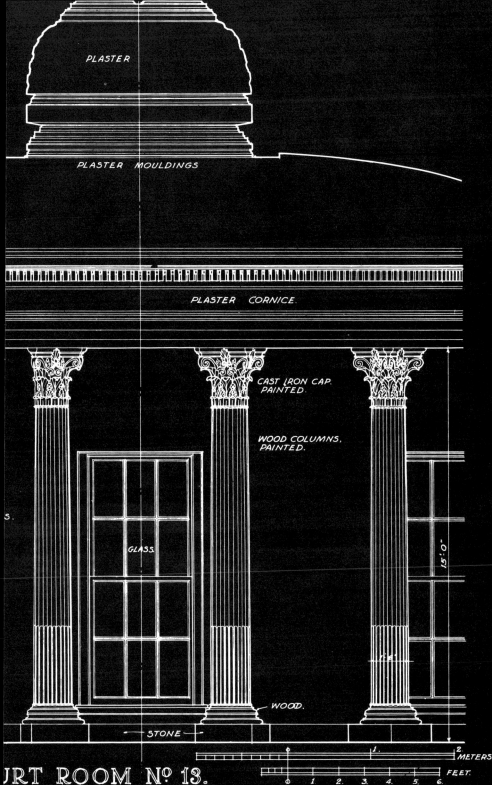

PLASTER

PLASTER MOULDINGS

PLASTER CORNICE.

CAST IRON CAP.
PAINTED.

WOOD COLUMNS,
PAINTED.

S.

GLASS.

15'0"

WOOD.

STONE

JRT ROOM № 13.

2. METERS

1. FEET.

0 1. 2. 3. 4. 5. 6.

The present building replaced a small brick courthouse that occupied the area now covered by the east
wing. The original courthouse had two stories, a
cupola, pillars in front, and was the most elegant
public building in the state. It was begun in 1826 and
completed in 1828. Until that time, the St. Louis
courts had been housed in a series of inadequate
quarters that included a Baptist church, three rooms
in Mr. Yosti's tavern, and the abandoned comman-
dant's house in the old Spanish fort.

The courthouse square originally was part of St.
Louis' common field located at the western edge of
the village. The land was later owned and donated to
the county as a courthouse site by Auguste Chouteau,
one of the city's founders, and Judge John B. C.
Lucas, who was among the original American officials appointed by President Jefferson to administer
the new Louisiana Territory. Before construction of
the first courthouse, the only object in the square was
a whipping post which had been there for many years.

In the decade following completion of the first
courthouse the population of St. Louis trebled, and
the county again was pressed to find more room for
its expanding activities. A contest was announced for
the best design for a new courthouse, with a first prize
of one hundred dollars and second prize of seventy
dollars. (This is curiously predictive of the great contest over a century later, first prize fifty thousand
dollars, that would result in the Gateway Arch, today
the Old Courthouse's companion structure in Jefferson National Expansion Memorial.) The contest was
held and the prizes awarded, but for some reason the
county officials did not build either winning design. A
while later they accepted instead a plan by Henry
Singleton that proposed to begin with an addition to
the small brick courthouse, then several stages finally
resulting in a Greek-porticoed, four-winged structure
with a low dome in the center. His design reflected the
prevailing architectural style of mid-nineteenth century known as Greek Revival, which contained several elements. One was the classical education of the
time. Another was the era's revived interest in arch-
eology, and an admiration for the Greek people who
recently had won their independence from the Turks.
Most significant, perhaps, was the kinship felt by the
young American Republic for the ancient Greek
Democracy.

18

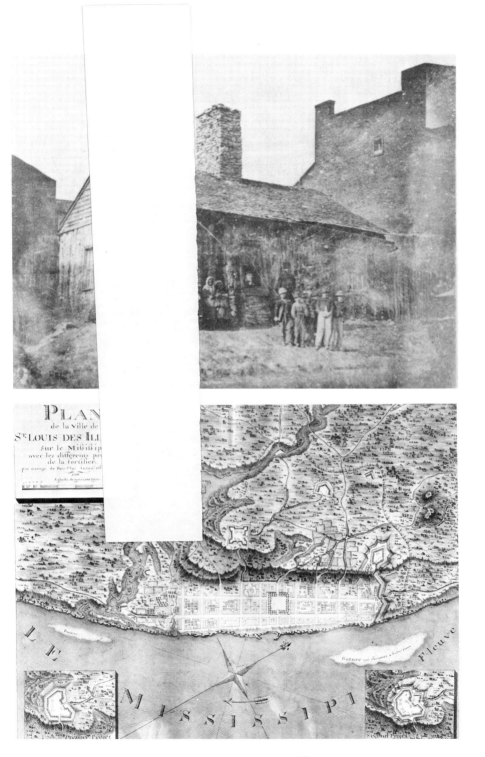

The plans for the first courthouse, drawn by Morton & Leveille, architects. This was the finest building in the state of Missouri when it was finished in 1828, at a cost of about $15,000; but it was soon outgrown by the rapidly swelling frontier town. The original plans were still in existence in 1928 when these pictures were made, but can no longer be found. Courtesy Jefferson National Expansion Memorial

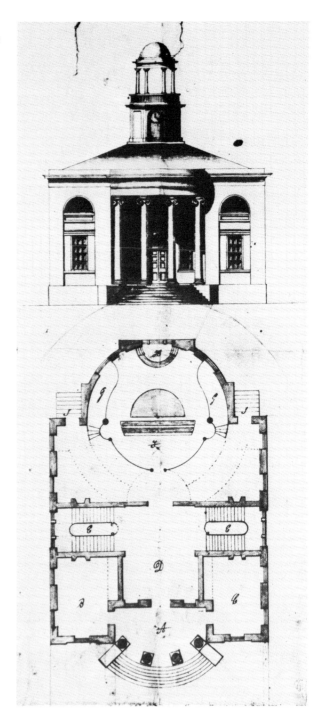

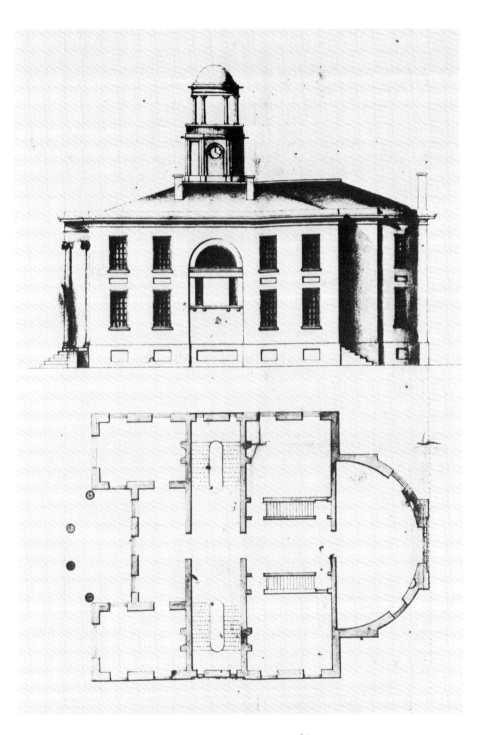

21

Right: *By 1822 St. Louis had
expanded far beyond the
borders shown on the 1796
map (p. 19): now the
courthouse site (cross-hatched
block) is well within the town.*
Above: *The view in 1840 from
the courthouse square
eastward. The old cathedral
(the tower on the right) still
stands today, but all else has
changed. The domed building
in the center was the Baptist
church. All the buildings
down by the water are now
removed for the park around
Gateway Arch; East St. Louis
fills the other side. (It is*
*interesting to compare this
scene, and the map on p. 19,
with the present view on pp.
2-3.)* From a lithograph by
J. C. Wild in *The Valley of
the Mississippi Illustrated*
(1841). Both Courtesy
Missouri Historical Society.

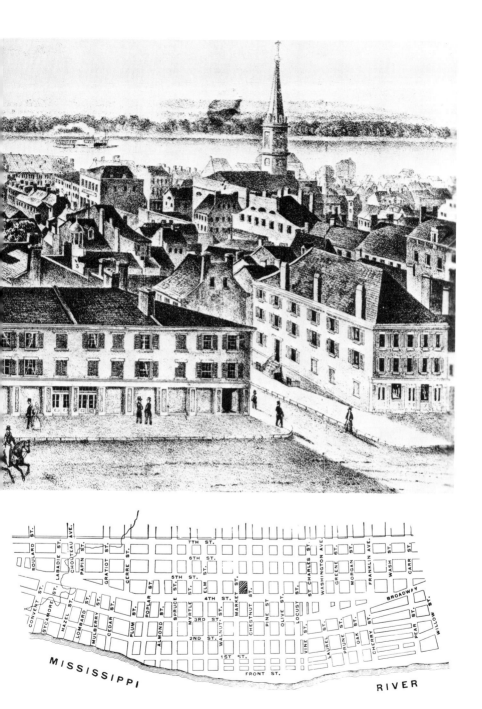

The cornerstone of the new courthouse was laid 21 October 1839. In attendance were the Masons, Odd Fellows, Hibernians, St. Louis Grays, and many citizens. The Hon. Wilson Primm gave the major address. Underneath the stone, in a sealed glass, were placed specimens of all St. Louis newspapers and United States coins, a copy of the program of the event, and a scroll listing the principal federal, state, and local officials of the day. The exact location of these objects today is unknown as the cornerstone has been hidden by subsequent construction.

The project did not proceed smoothly. The justices of the county court were bedeviled by a lack of funds, by what they considered incompetency on the part of their architects, and by a great deal of kibitzing from the newspapers and public. Major difficulties began in April of 1841 when it was found that the usual county revenues were not sufficient to carry on the work, thus forcing the court to seek a $30,000 loan. In January of the following year the justices fired Henry Singleton, the building's designer and first superintending architect, possibly because they thought he had been too extravagant with county funds. A dispute then arose between Singleton and the court as to how much the county owed him for past services.

Singleton's successor, William Twombly, lasted only eight months. The records do not reveal the cause of his dismissal, but previously he had been accused of allowing inferior work in the new jail for which he was also responsible. On his appointment, Twombly had been required to sign a $10,000 bond for "the faithful performance of the duties of his appointment." Whether Mr. Twombly was so unfortunate as to have to pay the county court $10,000 for the privilege of being fired is not known. In any case, the county again was in financial trouble. Most of the construction had to be suspended while the court sought a $75,000 loan. The president of the court even found it necessary to seek a loan for $2,000 under his own name to meet the day laborers' payroll.

On top of everything, the justices of the county court were berated by the public, the newspapers, and a grand jury demanding to know why the court was erecting an elegant palace for lawyers and judges while allowing other public facilities to deteriorate. The critics were especially incensed over the

24

deplorable condition of the county jail. The court disposed of this complaint by beginning a new jail, but it did not satisfy the riverboat men who had to slosh through mud on the unpaved wharf, or the county's farmers who were furious over the poorly maintained roads they were forced to use. When the grand jury asked the court about the road situation, the beleaguered justices declared that they did not have time to answer all the questions, a response that failed to satisfy the court's inquisitors.

There were some St. Louis citizens, of course, who were enthusiastically for the new building. One such civic booster, after showing a guest around the busy town, wrote, "When we reached the Court House now erecting, and, as I gazed upon it, there was a spark of pride arose in my bosom which enkindled into a lively flame and gave to my soul an importance as great as though I was viewing my own 'lordly possessions;' and for a moment I thought myself as rich as Cresis.... The country is able to pay for it—and is willing. Let it go on" (*Missouri Argus*, 11 June 1841). One wonders where his guest was from: the letter closes, "What city can boast of such improvements— can New York?—Philadelphia?—Baltimore?—*Cincinnati?*—NO!—Let the latter strike her colors and acknowledge Saint Louis as 'The Queen City of the West.' "

Amidst all the arguing, the actual construction continued with a fair degree of smoothness. Since the county was badly in need of space, the court assigned each new room as soon as it was usable. Part of the new building was occupied nearly three years before its official opening. The first sections completed were the short extensions which enclosed the rotunda on the north and south, each containing four small rooms. The first room was assigned to the probate judge as an office in April 1842. It was on the east side of the south extension on the ground floor. The original brick floor in this first room is still in place. Rooms on the north side of the rotunda were in use by October of that year.

The contractor had also made progress on the west wing. The exterior was substantially complete by the end of 1842. The latest products of an advancing industrial age were used in the building's construction. The roofs on the wings were among the first in the nation to be covered with galvanized iron. After the iron

The brick floor still visible in the connection to the east wing dates from 1842. Photo by Joseph Matthews: Courtesy Jefferson National Expansion Memorial

was laid, the county officials began to doubt its adequacy and paid $50 to have the new material chemically tested.

Work continued on the interior of the west wing, and in March 1843 the lower courtroom was ready for use. The court ordered final furnishings, consisting of chairs and a jury box, and assigned the room to the circuit court. The upper courtroom developed a sagging floor that delayed its opening until after the middle of the year.

The courtroom that was on the ground floor is of particular interest since it was the scene of the Dred and Harriet Scott case. The west wing has since been extensively remodeled and the original room obliterated, but various records give a general description of its appearance. The court records mention that the lower courtroom had a floor of pressed brick set on edge, and an editorial in the St. Louis *Daily People's Organ* of 25 January 1843 describes the nearly finished lower room as a "spacious and gorgeously furnished room, with its fluted columns and massive railings around the bar—its costly masonry and lofty ceilings with cornice and center circle..."

The writer also remarks on a number of elegantly styled desks inside the railing that were "covered with the finest sattinet, infinitely better than nineteen-twentieths of the tax-payers can afford to wear for pantaloons, and then the commodious drawer with the key, and we suppose the choicest stationary included."

These desks were assigned to lawyers by seniority. The younger members of the bar did not have any special accommodations. The editorial goes on to suggest that the desks be replaced with chairs and tables since under the present arrangement even the older attorneys had no place in the room where they could talk to their clients.

The writer also includes the inevitable remarks about the cost of the whole thing. The court must have anticipated this reaction to the ornate lower courtroom, for five days before the editorial appeared the justices instructed the contractor that the columns of the upper courtroom were to be "of the plainest kind and the seats in the galleries and lobbies to be plain pine benches with backs." The cost-cutting was not to be everywhere, though; the bar itself was to be the same as in the first-floor courtroom.

26

*Contemporary drawing of the
construction of the east wing,
about 1855.* Artist unknown:
Courtesy Jefferson National
Expansion Memorial

27

While the west wing was nearing completion, work also progressed on the rotunda. The exterior was finished about June 1843 with the raising of the copper-sheathed, wooden dome. Since Henry Singleton's original layout did not include a plan for the interior of the rotunda, the court accepted a design by George I. Barnett. Barnett already was familiar with the Courthouse, since after arriving from England in 1839 his first job had been to make a perspective drawing of the proposed building for Henry Singleton. The local architects at that time were unfamiliar with this drafting technique. The critical county court later had Barnett's design modified, and the rotunda interior was not completed until near the end of 1844.

The original rotunda lacked the mural work and ornate architectural detail of the present one, but observers of that era considered it impressive. The two upper balconies probably appeared much the same as they do now except that the supporting columns were of plain doric style. The first balcony extended in toward the center of the floor about eight feet farther than it does today and was supported by four massive one-piece stone pillars, instead of the present eight iron ones. An iron spiral stairway with an oak railing rose from the center of the floor and branched in two directions to the lower gallery. Six oil lamps on each balcony and one on each stone column on the ground floor provided illumination. The worn limestone slabs, about 3½ inches thick, that cover the present rotunda floor are the same ones laid in 1844. The whole scene was under the surveillance of an "eye" or round skylight in the center of the dome. The new building was officially opened on Washington's Birthday, 22 February 1845.

Civic pride in the new Courthouse, momentarily at least, eclipsed criticism of its cost. The *People's Organ* praised the architect and craftsmen for their work in building such a magnificent rotunda and such a "splendid piece of mechanism" as the spiral stairway. The newspaper further declared that because of the nation's westward expansion the city was bound to be the center of the country and if, as it hoped, St. Louis became the national capitol the Courthouse would make a fitting capitol building.

The *Saint Louis New Era* commented that the locust trees, sturdy brick sidewalks and beautiful wrought iron fence surrounding the Courthouse corresponded well with the building's own magnificence.

A visiting Scotsman noted the Courthouse's "common sense of plain clean, unpretending halls— fresh painted, airy and spacious." He was, however, surprised to find there were not any soldiers guarding the building, nor any armorial bearings on the walls.

The impressive new temple of justice was served by primitive utilities. The Courthouse purchased water from a public system which had been in existence since 1832. In the early years of operation, the water was not piped directly into the buildings. Instead, users had to draw their water from outdoor hydrants. The Courthouse was obtaining water in this manner as late as April 1853. The city water was supplemented by a pump already in use on the Courthouse grounds, and after the building was opened, a new well was dug at the southwest corner of the square. A public cistern also existed on the west side of the building. In June 1845 the court ordered that it "be altered in such manner that the fire engines of the City may be enabled to use their suction hoses in drawing water from it."

The city did not lay a sewer network until prompted by the cholera epidemic of 1849 and 1850. Accordingly, early court records show that David Hunt received $3 a week for sweeping the Courthouse's public privies once a day, Sundays excepted, and removing and cleaning the pans once each week.

St. Louis remained satisfied with its new Courthouse for less than four years. The editor of the *St. Louis Weekly Reveille,* in the 8 October 1848 issue, reminded his readers of the new building's unfinished condition and even insulted the old brick courthouse, comparing it to a fungus:

The Courthouse. *The bright sun is shining upon it revealing its proportions—deformed, unfinished. Its dome looks, phrenologically speaking, like a huge cranium upon a disproportionate body. The old building on Fourth Street appears to the eye like an unhealthy decaying fungus which had grown out from beneath its overshadowing neighbor. Loose pieces of marble lie scattered about the base of the building, whose antique front conveys a confused idea of age and ruin. There is an apparent struggle in its different parts, as if the modern march of*

The courthouse as it appeared about 1850, viewed from the southeast. The original courthouse is serving as the east wing, but with its cupola removed (see pp. 20-21). Daguerreotype by Emil Boehl: Courtesy Missouri Historical Society

improvement were laboring to usurp the place of the old and faded grandeur of past days.

By 1851 everyone agreed that it was time to complete the building. In the past ten years the city's population had increased nearly five-fold. The Mexican War had extended the nation's boundaries to the Pacific, and the discovery of gold had started a rush to California. St. Louis, located at the mouth of the Missouri, the "highway to the West," had become ever more important as a gateway and emporium to the West; she deserved a fine courthouse. The second stage of construction was planned and initiated by Robert S. Mitchell, who more than anyone was responsible for the Courthouse's present appearance. St. Louis, now a cosmopolitan city, did not lack for capable architects. Mitchell won his position in competition with several local and out-of-town bidders, including George I. Barnett, the designer of the rotunda. Mitchell's perspective drawing of the proposed new courthouse received much favorable attention. (Ironically, it had been Barnett's perspective drawing that had secured him the contract for the first dome, now to be replaced.) The editor of the St. Louis *Daily Evening News* of 6 April 1855 was especially impressed: "The picture is surpassingly beautiful and encourages our drooping hopes, for we really were beginning to think that the workmen on the building were so many Sysiphi, whose duty it was to hoist building stones to the top of the edifice for the sole purpose of pitching them down again."

Work began with demolition of the 1828 courthouse which, minus its cupola, had served as the east wing. It was hoped that the new wing would be opened in two years, but the usual construction, labor, and financial difficulties delayed its opening an additional two years. The east wing must have been ready for use early in 1856, for in March of that year the court authorized payment for the delivery of spittoons and other sundries for the new rooms.

The east wing contains one of the oldest and most interesting features in the building. It is an iron stairway which was constructed in about 1854. It has been in continuous use since that time. It spirals thirty-two feet from the first to the third floor without support from beneath. Its weight is carried entirely by the wall in which it is embedded.

The remarkable iron stairway in the east wing. Built about 1854, it has no vertical braces, but is supported solely by the wall in which it is embedded. It is still in constant use.
Photos by Joseph Matthews: Courtesy Jefferson National Expansion Memorial

By 1854 the courthouse (as it appears on pp. 30-31) was outgrown. Architect Robert Mitchell drew this picture of the proposed final courthouse. The picture drew much favorable comment, and Mitchell got the job of finishing the building.
Courtesy Jefferson National Expansion Memorial

36

Another notable feature in the new east wing was the iron frame for the roof. Along with the roof frame of the contemporary National Capitol Building in Washington, D.C., this was one of the first of its kind in the United States. The new roof was covered with copper. The frames and sheathing of the later wings would be constructed of the same materials.

The large oval courtroom on the second floor of the east wing still remains. The present arrangement of the furniture, however, dates from about 1905, and the judge's bench, court clerk's desk and bailiff's stand that visitors see today probably were built at this time.

Each new wing of the building required over four years to complete, but the total time was reduced by working on more than one wing at a time. The south extension was begun in 1853 and completed in 1858. Two of its first tenants were the state supreme court and the law association library.

In 1857 Robert Mitchell resigned, apparently because the court had awarded the stone contractor a substantial additional payment over Mitchell's protest. His successor, Thomas D. P. Lanham, gave the enemies of the county court the opportunity they had long awaited. Lanham was not a professional architect but a contractor who had been engaged at the Courthouse. Further, he was a brother of Phil Lanham, one of the justices of the court. To make things worse, Lanham's firm, under direction of his partner, Finfrock, continued its work on the building after his appointment as superintending architect. The newspapers and public did not fail to note these irregularities. The public outcry that followed caused the state legislature to abolish the county court and replace it with another administrative body called the Board of County Commissioners.

Between 1855 and 1860 the west wing was extensively remodeled, so much so that the only original parts of this section in existence today are the foundations and outer walls. The six-columned Grecian portico was added in front, making this the only wing that was ever completed essentially as Henry Singleton had planned it. The original roof was in dangerous condition so a new wrought iron roof frame was built and covered with copper. (The original covering had been galvanized iron.) At the same time the builders laid new fireproof floors in the wing.

This page and opposite: *The east courtroom, second floor, as it appears today. This room, completed in 1856, has been restored. The furnishings were built in 1905.* Photos by Joseph Matthews: Courtesy Jefferson National Expansion Memorial

37

This page and opposite: *The west courtroom, second floor. When this room was finished in 1843 it was quite plain, due to a public outcry over the ornateness—and expense—of the previously finished courtroom beneath it (p. 26). However about 15 years later it was remodeled, and today is restored to its 1860 appearance. The bench, railing, and other furnishings, except for the tables and chairs, are original.* Photos by Joseph Matthews: Courtesy Jefferson National Expansion Memorial

During this same period the west upper courtroom was rebuilt. The new room, with its massive central railing and stately columns, was the handsomest room in the building, and today is restored to its 1860 appearance. All of the furnishings, except for chairs and tables, are original.

In March 1855 the large, ornate circuit courtroom on the ground floor, scene of the Dred and Harriet Scott case and the oldest courtroom in the building, was demolished. The present corridor was run through the center of the room, thereby creating two smaller rooms on either side.

Construction began on the north wing in 1857 and finished in 1862. The officials had their usual problems. Work had to be interrupted while the brick contractor was fired and another hired, but the wing was nearly complete by December 1861. It served as the St. Louis City Hall from then until the fall of 1873.

During erection of the new wings, the newspapers continued to needle the county authorities for the slow rate of progress. Even a Memphis editor joined the chorus, writing, "The Court House, which has been in construction for three or four hundred years and which is really a fine building is still in process of erection. I am told that its first architect has been dead some two hundred years."

Other writers, however, reminded their readers that the city's unexpected, rapid growth was largely to blame for the difficulties connected with the building's development. The editor of the St. Louis *Missouri Republican,* writing in the 4 September 1859 issue, had his hopes raised somewhat when he saw the first supporting columns for the new dome rise against the skyline: "This relic is getting along. The pillars of the west wing are up and the cornice will be on some of these days. The first castings of the iron dome were raised yesterday, and placed on the rim of that immense perpendicular stone cylinder which has so long reminded us of a big lime kiln. Generations now alive may yet see the Court House completed."

The Courthouse watchers had agreed that the building needed a taller, more decorative dome when they had seen the old, low dome steadily skewed out of proportion by the extension of the wings. Robert Mitchell had depicted a new dome in his 1854 sketch of the future building, but the detailed design and engineering were accomplished by Lanham's successor,

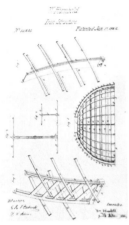

William Rumbold, between 1859 and 1862. The new dome was of Italian-Renaissance style. Prominent predecessors of this type were St. Peter's Cathedral in Rome and St. Paul's in London. The larger dome of the National Capitol Building was under construction at the same time. The iron skeletons of the St. Louis and Washington domes were unique in the United States, and were among the first in the world. They were to be repeated in the many similar domes crowning state capitols and other public buildings throughout the land. The designers of the statehouses took their inspiration from the National Capitol, but the St. Louis dome was completed 1½ years before, and in this sense, is the forerunner of those that followed.

Construction of the dome was delayed by a controversy over the adequacy of its iron bracing. Before being dismissed, Lanham had designed his own dome which Rumbold considered too heavy. Until that time iron had been little used as a building material on such a scale, and the city's architects were divided over the merits of the two designs. Rumbold was supported by Robert Mitchell; Lanham had the backing of Henry Singleton, the building's first architect, who insisted that the foundations were more than adequate for Lanham's heavier cast iron dome. He wrote, "The clay in which the foundations are layed is hard and dry. The foundation stones are of large dimensions, five and six feet below the surface of the ground, laid in cement of sufficient thickness to give beds for the succeeding courses. Each course is well grouted. The brick walls to the apex of the roof of the wings are laid with hard burned brick, with thin joints, and grouted every three or four courses, so that there is a perfect concrete from the foundation stone to the top brick."

The controversy was finally settled when Rumbold built a small scale model of his lighter wrought and cast iron dome and loaded it with 13,000 pounds of pig iron to convince the skeptics of its soundness. A contract for erection of Rumbold's dome was let in January 1860, and the exterior work was finished by April 1861.

(Today, with the Courthouse surrounded by taller buildings, it seems unlikely that we will see so remarkable a sight as lightning striking the copper-sheathed dome. But it has happened. The *Daily Democrat* for 8 April 1862 reports, "During the thunderstorm at about ten o'clock last night, a bolt

of lightning struck the Court House dome and was conducted by the safety rods to the earth. Persons who saw the dome at the instant represent the sight as indescribably brilliant and beautiful,—the vivid light playing over the entire surface of the dome.'')

Although neither the north wing nor the interior of the rotunda was yet complete, the Board of County Commissioners felt a great sense of accomplishment on seeing their new dome towering 190 feet over the city, and felt that some kind of ceremony should mark its completion. On 6 June 1861 about fifteen men led by John H. Lightner, president of the board, climbed to the summit of the dome and placed several appropriate articles in the gold ball atop the cupola. These included the names of persons connected with the construction, several local newspapers, a twenty-five cent piece, and an ink bottle with silver pen used in recording the names of those in attendance.

The Courthouse builders succeeded in constructing a new rotunda that matched the dignified beauty of the building's exterior. Architect and muralist collaborated to create a striking but tasteful whole in an age often noted for excessive ornamentation. The original doric columns that supported the two upper balconies were removed and replaced with more ornate ionic and corinthian pillars. (Those columns that bear a structural load are iron, while the merely decorative ones are of wood, made to look alike. You can tell them apart easily by tapping on them.) The builders created a fourth gallery at the base of the new dome and enclosed it with an iron railing. The lantern or cupola on top was not originally glassed in. Instead, separating the base of the cupola from the rotunda interior was a round skylight similar to that on the first dome. Architect Rumbold also removed from the center of the rotunda the spiral stairway that had been little used since the installation of stairways in the wings.

The most arresting features in the new rotunda were the murals depicting historical scenes and personages, and allegorical figures. They were done under contract with August Becker. Associated with Becker was his half-brother, Charles Wimar. Wimar painted nine-foot symbolic figures titled ''Justice,'' ''Law,'' ''Liberty,'' and ''Commerce'' in the twenty-three foot vertical recesses in the dome, and four historical vignettes in the crescent-shaped lunettes. Of

Above: *The fourth gallery, highest in the rotunda, added with the new dome.* Photo by Joseph Matthews: Courtesy Jefferson National Expansion Memorial

Opposite: *The view from the southeast in 1866, shortly after completion of the dome. The building has almost assumed its final exterior appearance, although the cupola is not yet glassed in.* Courtesy Jefferson National Expansion Memorial.

Previous page: *Looking down from the cupola to the stone floor, 190' below.* Photo by Joseph Matthews: Courtesy Jefferson National Expansion Memorial

Opposite: *Looking up into the rotunda.* Courtesy Dorrill Photographers

this original mural work, completed near the end of 1862, only the lunettes remain today, and they have been altered extensively.

Charles Wimar was born near Bonn, Germany, and brought to St. Louis in 1843 when fifteen years of age. He began his career as an apprentice to Leon Pomarede who may have encouraged him to pursue an interest in Indians. He later returned to Germany where he remained four years studying his craft. After returning to St. Louis, Wimar made two extensive trips up the Missouri River to further familiarize himself with the western country and its Indian inhabitants. Wimar, acknowledged as more accomplished than either his half-brother or former teacher, was given the task of designing the entire Courthouse mural scheme. He might have done more of the actual painting had he not been seriously ill with tuberculosis. Tradition says that he had to be carried to the platform each day, and a mattress placed next to him so that he might rest at regular intervals. He died at the age of thirty-four, just months after finishing the murals.

Wimar's four lunettes relate to the history of St. Louis. Each is placed in the direction of the event it portrays. On the south quadrant of the rotunda is the Spanish explorer de Soto discovering the Mississippi River near present Memphis in 1541. The east lunette depicts Pierre Laclede, with thirteen year old Auguste Chouteau at his side, founding St. Louis in February 1764. The site, previously selected by Laclede, was the closest place to the mouth of the Missouri which was safe from flooding. Laclede's keelboat is supposed to be accurately rendered. Before starting the mural, Wimar interviewed an aged Frenchman who as a boy had seen the vessel on many occasions. Artistic license was used in including Laclede and the Indians, however. Laclede did not arrive until April, having sent young Chouteau ahead with thirty men to direct construction of the first buildings. Indians were not on hand to greet the explorers, although eight months later a band of Missouris arrived to investigate the landing.

The north lunette recreates the unsuccessful British-Indian assault on Spanish-held St. Louis in 1780. The action occurred during the American Revolution after Spain had become allied with the colonies. The scene may be fairly accurate, but the

46

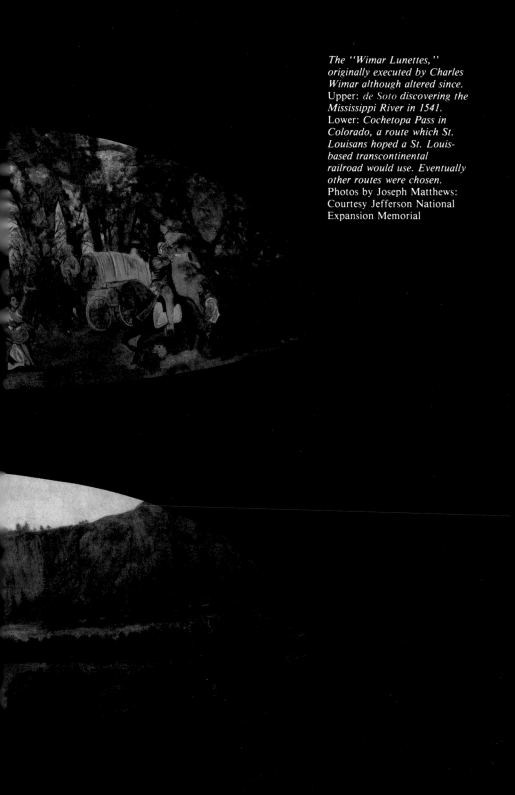

*The "Wimar Lunettes,"
originally executed by Charles
Wimar although altered since.*
Upper: *de Soto discovering the
Mississippi River in 1541.*
Lower: *Cochetopa Pass in
Colorado, a route which St.
Louisans hoped a St. Louis-
based transcontinental
railroad would use. Eventually
other routes were chosen.*
Photos by Joseph Matthews:
Courtesy Jefferson National
Expansion Memorial

Upper: *The British-Indian attack on St. Louis during the American Revolution, 1780.* Lower: *The founding of St. Louis: Pierre Laclede coming ashore.* *See text for comments on the historial authenticity of these scenes.* Photos by Joseph Matthews: Courtesy Jefferson National Expansion Memorial

high log wall had not yet been built around the village, and only one stone tower was near completion.

Cochetopa Pass is shown in the west lunette. This pass in the Colorado Rockies, although never used, was at one time important to Missouri as a possible way through the mountains for a proposed St. Louis to San Francisco railroad. Missouri's Senator Thomas Hart Benton, often speaking in this building, strongly backed a route through this pass. All four of Wimar's historical lunettes have undergone extensive modification, as will be described.

The plasterers and woodworkers deserve credit for their work on the rotunda, particularly the unknown craftsman who created the Missouri state seals at the base of the dome below the vertical figures. These remain in near-perfect condition today.

By July 1862, the exterior of the building had reached its present appearance and the rotunda nearly so. At that time the total construction cost came to $1,199,871.91. This was in an era when laborers received $1 a day, and the superintending architect $125 per month. A further cost was the life of Conrad Stousanback who was crushed to death by one of the dome's iron ribs. The county granted his widow a quarterly allowance of $20.

Alterations were made in the building's interior in 1870. The first balcony was cut back about eight feet to its present dimensions, and the four supporting stone columns were removed and replaced with eight iron columns. The plain appearance of the new ground floor columns is in sharp contrast to the rest of the rotunda. This may be part of the general scheme of increasing complexity as one goes upward (each rank of pillars is more decorated than the one below it), or it may indicate that the lower pillars were at one time hidden by an arcade, or sheathed in some way. The replaced stone pillars were purchased by Henry Shaw for use in his landscaping of Tower Grove Park, and presently stand at the park's Tower Grove Avenue entrance. The large, square base stones for these columns are still visible in the rotunda floor. Also in 1870 skylights were placed in the large oval courtrooms on the second floor, while the skylight at the top of the dome was removed and the cupola provided with glass instead. These alterations were made by Architect Thomas W. Walsh who succeeded William Rumbold after his death in 1867.

The 1862 Courthouse had more modern facilities. Water was now piped directly into the building, although a pump was still in use as late as 1872. Gas lighting was installed in 1853. The lamps presently seen on the third and fourth galleries are original gas fixtures wired for electricity. Central steam heating replaced coal burning stoves in 1870. The new heating system immediately drew a swarm of complaints. The St. Louis *Daily Democrat* of 8 January 1871 states that neighbors of the Courthouse were incensed over the foul smelling clouds of thick, black smoke that boiled out of the building's furnace. The noxious smoke was caused by burning soft coal, and the situation was the same all over St. Louis and other American cities, since most buildings used the same heating method. This would become an increasing problem in St. Louis until the 1930s, when effective laws finally put an end to that form of pollution.

The same newspaper on 29 December 1870 describes a further problem with the heating system: "The heating coils in the County Court room furnished heat enough to roast the jurors and judges, while there is not enough in the Marshal's office to warm a Laplander in June."

At least the steam coils were more pleasing to the eye than the stoves they replaced. The architect of the large oval courtroom on the second floor of the west wing had solved the aesthetic problem by hiding the stoves in small corner rooms vented to heat the larger room. These vented closets still can be seen. Probably the most welcome improvement was the introduction of a modern sewage disposal system in 1851, prompted by the cholera epidemic of two years before.

The county authorities also gave attention to the Courthouse grounds. In 1858 they ordered a sundial for the southeast corner of the yard. This is the only outdoor feature which has remained to the present. (The existing fountain and iron fence are copies of those that appeared in the 1860s with the completed building.) The Courthouse of this period was also graced by elm trees along the curbs—and a turtle which resided in the basin of the fountain. The little creature has been fittingly immortalized in iron on the gates of the restored Courthouse fence. In its day, it won distinction as the only thing connected with the building that did not require an appropriation of the

55

taxpayers' money! The turtle was donated by custodian James Quigley, who was one of those amusing characters of whom newspaper writers take notice. Once both he and the turtle achieved the status of being mentioned in a poem in the *Daily Democrat* of 13 April 1872:

When Spring with dewy fingers cold
Returns to deck the Courthouse mould,
She there shall find the fountain sealed
and Quigley's turtle 'ausgespealed'.

In another instance, Quigley selected a red, white and green carpet for the county courtroom. The red, he said, was to match the red tape of the court, the white matched the dingy white color of the building, and the green was to remind the county officials of the grass he had to cut by hand. Four years later a newspaper item reveals that the unlucky Quigley was still shaving the Courthouse lawn by hand. In 1869 a salesman with a "patented lawn mowing machine" came by and cut Quigley's grass for him. Bystanders were so impressed they got up a petition (very likely at Quigley's instigation) requesting that the county purchase a mower for the hardworking custodian. The frugal county officials declined the plea.

In 1873 the flagpole which had been fixed to the apex of the cupola twelve years before broke off and crashed through a skylight. The loud noise caused a great deal of alarm among the inhabitants of the Courthouse, who, no doubt, suddenly recalled the architects' heated controversies over the strength of the new iron dome. The event is well described by the *St. Louis Democrat* of 25 September:

Stampede at the Court House—Fall of the Flag Staff. *A day or two ago the admirers of Father Marquette applied to the County Court for permission to hoist the American flag over the Court-house in honor of the "discovery of the Mississippi River by the adventurous missionary, 200 years ago." The court, glad to learn that the honor of the discovery of the great river was due to a French priest, instead of a bloody Spaniard, as history falsely records, willingly issued the order to have the flag raised on yesterday morning. In addition to this cheap display, the court granted permission to the great American illuminator, Captain*

Butts, of the Grand Opera House, to illuminate the dome with his celebrated calcium lights. In accordance with the programme and the order of the court, as soon as the sun rose on the 200th anniversary of Marquette's great discovery the flag was hoisted to the peak of the flagstaff. The heavens were not propitious and did not smile upon the flag. On the contrary, the clouds lowered, and the rain descended, soaking the starry flag with moisture. About 10 o'clock, when the lawyers had gathered in the petitions, a crash of glass was heard in the vicinity of the dome, sounding like the "wreck of matter and the crush of worlds." No one had any idea of the cause of the disturbance, but the first thought was that the Old Court-house was crumbling to pieces. Lawyers rushed in alarm from the court room; clerks threw down their pens and sought places of safety, while the janitor stood paralyzed with fear. One of the Comptroller's clerks, who has always escaped military duty on account of a stiff knee, made better time than any one else, and reached the opposite side of the street in three bounds. The fire alarm telegraph operators, over whose heads the crash was loudest, supposed the dome was struck by lightening, and lost no time in making a "ground connection" with the street. The sheriff's deputies huddled in a corner, like sheep at the appearance of a wolf, and knew not whether to flee. In a few moments the alarm subsided, and it was discovered that the strong wind blowing from the southwest had snapped the flag staff short off within three feet of the butt, and it had fallen over the side of the dome into the skylight of the north wing. This was all. The damage was slight, and it will cost $200 or $300 to have a new flag staff made and put up. The next one ought to be of iron. The old pole was found to be rotten and cracked, and its downfall was only a question of time. This mishap did not prevent Captain Butts from touching off his calcium lights, last night and while the celebration was going on at the German's Club the Court-house was in a blaze of glory in honor of the discovery of the Upper Mississippi.

By 1880 moisture and grime had taken their toll on the murals, and it was decided to have them retouched or redone. August Becker would have been the logical choice for the work but he was engaged elsewhere.

Allegorical figures from the
dome, painted by Ettore
Miragoli in 1880. The original
Wimar paintings that filled
these spaces apparently were
removed; recent tests indicate
that they are irrecoverable.
Clockwise from upper left:
"History," "Knowledge,"
"Law," and "Instruction."
Photos by Joseph Matthews:
Courtesy Jefferson National
Expansion Memorial

The city authorities (the building was now under city jurisdiction) engaged a resident Italian muralist, Ettore Miragoli. If judged on the basis of enthusiasm and quantity alone, a better artist could not have been found. Miragoli, with the help of his crew, completely painted out Wimar's nine-foot figures in the dome, substituting similar subjects of his own design. He was about to demolish Wimar's lunettes when August Becker found out what he was doing and had him stopped by city authorities. When questioned about this action, Miragoli declared that his talents were superior to Wimar's or anyone else who had received the bulk of his training in the United States.

The condition of the original murals before Miragoli began his renovations is not exactly known, but judging from Becker's actions when he heard they were to be removed, and Miragoli's opinion of American-trained artists, it can be surmised that they did not deserve complete removal.

In addition to the above work, Miragoli frescoed the remaining vacant spaces in the rotunda. Virtually all of the present mural work, with the exception of the lunettes, is his.

In the small upper dome, just below the cupola, are eight more paintings originally done by Miragoli. These were in poor condition when the National Park Service acquired the Courthouse. The present ones are copies of the originals, because the plaster was so deteriorated that it could not be retained. Four are portraits of Columbus, Lincoln, John Adams, and Ulysses Grant. The remaining four are allegorical compositions representing "Agriculture," "Commerce," "Administration," and "The United States." Below these, in the four vertical recesses once occupied by Wimar's work, are symbolic female figures representing "Knowledge" (Northeast), "History" (Northwest), "Instruction" (Southwest), and "Law" (Southeast).

Immediately below the Missouri State seals are four additional portraits by Miragoli. These depict Frank P. Blair (southwest), the leader of Union forces in St. Louis at the outbreak of the Civil War; Andrew Johnson (northwest), Lincoln's vice-president and the seventeenth president of the United States; Hernando deSoto (northeast), the discoverer of the Mississippi River; and Daniel Webster, the prominent American statesman and orator.

Under each of the above portraits, between the lunettes, Miragoli painted cartouches, apparently civic symbols, featuring eagles and cherubs.

Below these, in the vertical panels on the third balcony, the Italian artist rendered four women in classic garb symbolizing "Administration," "The Republic," "Diligence," and "Constancy." So far as can be determined Miragoli never mentioned which was which. The first two are easily distinguished from the latter two, but the distinction between "Republic" and "Administration" on the one hand, and "Diligence" and "Constancy" on the other is not obvious. Readers are invited to test their interpretive skills on these figures.

Below the lunettes are four portraits, probably by Miragoli. They depict George and Martha Washington (west and north) and Thomas Hart Benton and Edward Bates (east and south). Benton was a renowned senator from Missouri for thirty years. Bates, a leading public figure in St. Louis, was attorney general in Lincoln's first cabinet.

The lunettes were not the best of Wimar's work. This is understandable considering the artist's physical condition at the time they were done, and the fact that he was unfamiliar with fresco techniques. Nevertheless, Wimar's stature had grown since his death, and the city officials wished to preserve his work in the Courthouse. Miragoli had not been permitted to touch the lunettes in 1880, although undoubtedly they needed attention. By 1888 their peeling condition was easily noticed from the ground floor. In that year the city hired August Becker to repair his half-brother's work. In 1905 the lunettes were retouched again by Professor Edmund Wuerpel of Washington University's School of Fine Arts. But by 1921 the murals, still ravaged by dampness and dirt, once more needed attention. The city entrusted their restoration to James Lyons, an employee of a commercial painting and decorating firm. Instead of restoring the murals, however, Lyons, like Miragoli before him, proceeded to superimpose his own creations. It was not long before the newspapers discovered this.

The hapless artist, innocent in the belief that he was only helping to restore the rotunda to its original beauty, suddenly found himself, and the city official who had employed him, the targets of an outraged

Ettore Miragoli's allegorical figures above the third balcony. Probably they are "The Republic" (Upper left), *"Administration"* (Upper right), *"Constancy"* (Lower left), *and "Diligence." These identifications are tentative based on symbolisms, as Miragoli did not label the panels.* Photos by Joseph Matthews: Courtesy Jefferson National Expansion Memorial

The portraits of historical figures beneath the lunettes, originally by Ettore Miragoli. They are, clockwise from upper left: Thomas Hart Benton; George Washington; Edward Bates; and Martha Washington. When the National Park Service began restoration of the rotunda in 1955 the portraits were found to be deteriorated beyond repair; these are reproductions. Photos by Joseph Matthews: Courtesy Jefferson National Expansion Memorial

citizenry. The controversy is summarized in *St. Louis Post-Dispatch* editorials of 15 and 17 October:

Mayor Kiel's Duty. *Will Mayor Kiel permit the vandal work that is being done in the Courthouse dome to continue, as Mr. McKelvey says it will, because the city has a contract with a firm of house painters? Mayor Kiel should take the matter in hand and call upon the Municipal Art Commission or appoint a competent committee to see if it is possible to restore the Wimar paintings from destruction. It is clearly the Mayor's duty to save the City further loss from the blundering of his appointee in the Department of Public Safety. It ought not be possible for such a costly mistake to be made. . . .*

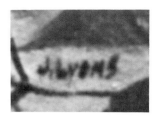

Signature of *"J. Lyons"* on a painting originally by Wimar. Studies in 1955 revealed this signature, although it had been painted over. Courtesy Jefferson National Expansion Memorial

Director of Public Safety McKelvey who has charge of public buildings, said today that he would order the removal of the signature 'J. Lyons, '21' from the painting of The Landing of Laclede at the Site of St. Louis *and from any any other Wimar's paintings that had been so marked. He also said he would prohibit any work on the four allegorical panels by Wimar on the fourth floor which have not yet been 'retouched' by James Lyons.*

He has called a meeting of the Missouri Historical Society and the Municipal Art Commission for October 24. Mr. McKelvey was asked what he thought of the artistic skill of Lyons compared to that of Wimar. He replied: "Who was this Wimar? Nobody ever heard of him until his painting these pictures. I don't think he was much of an artist or he would have put them on canvas instead of on the plaster which fell off in places."

Lyons admitted that he had made the coloring in one of the historical paintings too bright (The Attack on St. Louis in 1780) *but he resented any other criticism.*

Apparently Director of Public Safety McKelvey, referring here to the four allegorical panels "by Wimar," did not know that they already had been at least painted over, and possibly removed first, by Miragoli. In any case, Lyons finally was stopped, but not before he had altered the lunettes considerably.

A Public Forum

The Courthouse rotunda once was one of the largest rooms in St. Louis, and for many years served as the city's public forum. In a time when commercial amusement was limited, public events were well attended, and oratory was developed into a fine art. If the speaker had a reputation as an accomplished orator and if the subject was of sufficient interest, his audience might fill the ground floor and all three balconies. If a parade was part of the affair or if the rotunda proved too small for all of those who wished to attend, the crowd would gather outside while the speaker gave his address from the east portico.

St. Louis praised the rotunda as generally well suited to public gatherings. One inconvenience, however, was the spiral stairway in the center. This was discussed in an editorial in the *St. Louis Missouri Republican* of 2 May 1855:

But will the architect of the Court House permit us to make a suggestion? Would it not be well to remove the spiral stairs in the Rotunda, and in their place open side entrances from the halls to the galleries above? We do not know but this improvement is already contemplated among the rearrangements decided upon. The difficulties which attend these stairways are suggestive enough, it must be admitted. Let them be removed, and a great deal more room will be added to the Rotunda; for the lower floor would then be given to the area. As it is, no one can see or hear anything from below. The steps become immediately jammed, affording as they do a near position to the speaker, and the dense mass obstructs all view and all distinct articulation. They do more than this: for long before the seats are filled in the second and third tiers, all ingress is prevented, without great labor and the risk of disturbance, by the crowd congregated on them.

The Rotunda, with this exception, is well adapted to popular assemblies. No room of the same dimensions in the city is better suited to the voice. In the upper tiers every word uttered with common force is plainly distinguishable. These spiral steps are offensive to the eye as well. They mar the architectural harmony of the Rotunda, and sadly incommode the passage-way through the main body of the building. The addition of the two wings will render this fault more apparent than ever. Take this away, therefore,

66

*and open entrances on either side of the Rotunda
—one for ascending and the other for descending—
and we shall have a place of ample dimensions for
public meetings, where all may hear distinctly and
nearly all be seen, and where, in the passage of the
citizens in and out, up and down, all necessary order
and quiet may be observed.*

Judging from the above account, the speaker's customary place was on the first balcony, or, perhaps, on top of the spiral stairway. The criticisms may have been justified; at any rate the staircase would be removed in 1862.

The first public event in the Courthouse was the building's official opening ceremony held on Washington's Birthday, 22 February 1845. The ground floor, the three balconies, and the stairway were packed for the occasion. The two upper tiers were reserved for the ladies who presented "a thick-set galaxy of beauty and fashion." On the ground floor were bands and handsomely uniformed militia. Uriel Wright, the most eloquent orator in the state, gave the major address—"such a one as Washington himself would have approved." The program concluded with the singing of the *Star Spangled Banner* "in a manner rarely excelled."

The opening ceremonies advertised the building's virtues and availability as a public meeting place. Only a week later Kemper Medical College, the first such school west of the Mississippi, held its commencement exercises in the rotunda. The young physicians being graduated would be badly needed four years later when cholera ravaged the city.

The period 1840 to 1860 was the time of the great westward migrations, of the Mexican War, of railroad building, of rising tensions between North and South, and of waves of foreign immigration sparked by famine in Ireland and revolution in Germany. Each of these events was the subject of meetings held at the Courthouse.

Between 1841 and 1869, before rails spanned the continent, three hundred fifty thousand persons set out across the plains by wagon for Oregon, California, and other points west. St. Louis was a major outfitting point. Settlers and goldseekers embarked from here by riverboat or wagon for the "jumping off places" along the Missouri River between present day

Kansas City and Omaha. One typical group of west-
bound emigrants met at the Courthouse in response to
an advertisement that appeared in the *St. Louis Daily
Peoples' Organ* of 5 April 1843:

Emigrants to Oregon. *All persons intending to emigrate to Oregon are requested to meet at the Court
House (in conjunction with the citizens friendly to the
cause) on Thursday evening next, the 7th inst., at half
past seven o'clock.*

*The Committee of Vigilance earnestly request all
persons desiring to emigrate, to hand in their names,
previous to the above called meeting, to either of the
following persons:*
James Makin, Collins St., rear of Broadway Cottage.
Miles Eyre, No. 72 North Second Street
L. Almer, corner of Plumb and South Second Streets
*Mr. Kimberly (jeweller) Oak St., between Second and
Third.*

*The Committee hope that particular attention will
be paid to this call, as it is absolutely necessary to
know the precise strength of the party, in order that
proper arrangements may be made for the comfort of
every person during its march. Those who cannot call
in person are requested to send in their names, but
where it is possible, each emigrant should call in person, as many arrangements must necessarily be made,
and perfect concert of action is indispensable. No in-
dividual bearing a bad character need make applica-
tion, as persons of that class will not be permitted
under any circumstances, to join the party.*

By order of the Committee of Vigilance
Miles Eyre, Chairman

News of the Mexican War reached St. Louis in
May 1846. For the next fourteen months the Courthouse was witness to waving flags, throbbing drums,
and patriotic oratory. The country was not unanimously for the conflict. Some regarded it as an
immoral assault on a weak neighbor and a plot by
southerners to gain more territory for slavery. But
most St. Louisans agreed with those who held that
if the United States did not occupy the Mexican
possessions some other army would, and above all, it
was the nation's destiny to extend its boundaries to
the Pacific. The newly opened rotunda was the scene
of several gatherings held to support the war. The

first was an immense rally to enlist troops for the coming battles. This was followed shortly by two more meetings to raise money for the families of the volunteers.

Missourians rushed to the colors with enthusiasm but with little advance planning. When unexpected numbers arrived in the city, emergency quarters had to be found. The rotunda was one of the places that served as a temporary barracks, and it must have been noisy.

After organization and provisioning in St. Louis, the volunteers headed for the seat of war. One major expedition, the Army of the West under General Stephen W. Kearny that marched to New Mexico, occupied that territory without a shot and then took California, had a large contingent of St. Louisans.

When the war was won and the soldiers were on their way home, citizens gathered in the rotunda to arrange a fitting welcome. The result of these meetings was a huge procession that formed on Fourth Street in front of the Courthouse and the Planters House Hotel. From here the participants marched to Camp Lucas on the western edge of the city (now Twelfth and Olive) where the ceremonies ended after a suitable speech by Senator Thomas Hart Benton.

The rotunda was the scene of more somber proceedings when funeral honors were paid Col. John J. Hardin and Lt. B. R. Houghton of the Illinois volunteers. Their coffins rested on a black-draped stage built over the circular railing that enclosed the spiral stairway. Muskets were stacked around the platform, and several small cannons and an American flag placed on top. An American flag and several state banners hung from the first balcony, and a garland of leaves was suspended from the top of the dome. The funeral atmosphere was heightened when Senator Benton gave the eulogy under a darkened skylight, in the faint illumination of lamps ranged along the rotunda walls.

During the 1840s and 1850s the rotunda saw several assemblies dealing with European problems and the resulting immigration into the United States. Basically there were two sources of hardship: famine in Ireland and revolution in Germany.

In Ireland, a series of cold, damp summers beginning in 1845 destroyed the potato crops. With that staple wiped out, nearly a quarter of the population

Robert Campbell, Irish immigrant who made a fortune in the fur trade. Photo by John A. Scholten: Courtesy Missouri Historical Society

perished. A son of northern Ireland in St. Louis named Robert Campbell had come here in 1824, become a famous mountain man and made a fortune in the fur trade. He had been a leader in marshaling St. Louis' resources in support of the Mexican War, and now he organized a meeting in the Courthouse to help in the Irish famine. (In 1851 he would visit his place of birth, and be honored with cannon salutes and triumphal arches for his efforts in relieving his kinsmen's suffering.)

But the famine was massive. Hundreds of thousands of unskilled, illiterate Irish poured into the large eastern cities. The native laboring class feared job competition from the foreigners, while the wealthier Americans resented higher police and welfare costs. Both groups protested the manner in which the newcomers were manipulated by big city political bosses. In some places, the bitterest issue between the Catholic-Irish and native Protestants was over Bible reading in the Protestant dominated public schools.

Given these ingredients, it is not surprising that violence occurred. The country's worst outbreak was in 1844 in Philadelphia, where an anti-Irish mob overwhelmed the police, repulsed the militia, and ruled the city for several days before being suppressed.

St. Louis, far from the eastern seaboard, was spared the worst effects of this social and religious unrest, but did not escape entirely. In 1854 anti-Irish rioting erupted during a city election. Thousands of "natives" and Irish battled with bricks and guns. The police were helpless. The militia companies were called out and managed to disperse the larger mobs but could not handle the small scattered groups that immediately formed and continued the violence.

Mayor John How suspended the regular police, and at an emergency meeting in the Courthouse enrolled a special force of seven hundred men. Many of these were prominent citizens who were to use their moral authority as well as force on the rioters. At this meeting the mayor urged all "parents, guardians and masters" to keep their "children, wards, and apprentices" in at night. The special police and military at last restored order, but ten people had been killed, many wounded and much property destroyed. Most of the violence and destruction was in the Irish section north of Washington Avenue, between the wharf and Eighth Street.

In Germany the trouble was not famine, but revolution. One of the largest, most spectacular assemblages ever to form at the Courthouse was a procession supporting the forces of liberalism in the German revolution of 1848. A multitude of all ages and both sexes filled the Courthouse yard and adjacent streets. The crowd met twice on 25 April, once during the day and again in the evening. The evening meeting was lit by two huge bonfires that blazed on Market and Chestnut Streets, and by five hundred torches held aloft. The affair began with a speech from the east portico of the building that was followed by shouts, the waving of flags, the firing of guns, and bursts of music from several bands. The crowd included units of armed men who had volunteered to join the European struggle.

In spite of this distant help, the revolution failed, and soon its refugees began arriving in the United States. Generally more highly skilled and educated than the Irish, they were better received. But these individuals were heirs of the French Revolution and many were outspokenly anti-religious, a trait that did not endear them to staunch, Protestant Americans. Furthermore, all Germans, of whatever degree of piety, loved to spend Sundays in their beer gardens. To many Americans, this was a desecration of the Sabbath.

Violence between Germans and native-born occurred in St. Louis in 1852. The immediate cause was alleged election fraud by the Germans. The rioting finally ended with the local militia dispersing a mob in front of the printing office of the German newspaper *Anzieger des Westerns*. No lives were lost, but at least ten persons were seriously injured.

On several occasions, large crowds gathered in the rotunda to hear calls for laws restricting immigration. Two of the most eloquent orators in the state were heard, Uriel Wright, keynote speaker at the Courthouse opening, and Dr. Joseph Nash McDowell, founder of Kemper Medical College. The restrictive legislation demanded in the 1840s was not passed until the 1920s.

The immigration story ended happily. Social unrest subsided as the newcomers became assimilated. The descendents of the immigrants are now, save for name, indistinguishable from the people (themselves descendents of earlier immigrants) who persecuted them. St. Louis culture was not over-whelmed, but enhanced. The melting pot worked.

The year 1849 was a full one in St. Louis history, with the Courthouse involved in it all. The city's wharf was crowded with steamboats, sometimes moored solid abreast and three deep, and her streets were crowded with "Forty-niners" hurriedly prepar-ing to become the Gold Rush to California. In the midst of all this came a murderous cholera epidemic, a fire that swept the city, and the year closed with the great railroad convention.

Cholera brought dread that sometimes verged on panic. The role of micro-organisms in causing disease was not then understood, and fear of cholera was fear of the unknown. Many people fled, including enough members of the city council to render local govern-ment inoperative. To deal with the crisis a mass meeting convened at the Courthouse on 25 June. The meeting resulted in the city government, with the mayor's approval, being virtually replaced with a special committee of twelve prominent citizens.

The committee ordered that school buildings be converted into hospitals, and that stone coal, resinous tar, and sulphur be burned on the street corners, hop-ing the smoke would dissipate or suppress the foul air that was thought to cause the sickness. The committee also enforced a quarantine against river traffic and set aside 2 July as a day of prayer and fasting.

Although the specific cause of the disease was still unknown, the medical authorities suspected some re-lationship between cholera and unclean water. The "noxious vapors" and "miasmas" that rose from stagnant pools were generally blamed.Consequently, at another Courthouse meeting, called by Mayor John M. Krum, it was recommended that a number of stagnant or sluggish water holes scattered about the city be drained and a sewer system built to prevent future accumulations. These bodies of water had been clean and pure originally, but in later years had become polluted with sewage and other filth. Most notable of these was Chouteau's Pond which for many years had been a place of recreation for the people of St. Louis. There was much sentiment against destroying one of the city's oldest and favorite features, but by then it was too late to return the pond to its original condition. Factories and butcher shops had multiplied along its banks, adding to its already

72

St. Louis was changing, from a village to a city. Part of the price for this was paid by the terrain the city spread across. Chouteau's Pond had been a favorite gathering place until increasing pollution ruined it. Today Union Station stands approximately where this pond was. Painting (c. 1844) by D. Barbier: Courtesy Missouri Historical Society

heavy load of pollution. By the time it was finally
obliterated in 1853, sentiment was all anyone could
have for Chouteau's Pond. In addition to specific
cases like Chouteau's Pond, following the cholera
epidemic a modern sewer network was begun and extended as the city grew.

One night in May, while the cholera epidemic and
the struggle against it were in full swing, a steamboat
at the wharf burst into flames. In spite of efforts to
control it the fire quickly spread to other steamboats,
and then ashore. It swept through the whole commercial district, approximately the area of the present
park surrounding Gateway Arch. The Courthouse escaped destruction, and the next day was the scene of a
mass meeting held to cope with the aftermath of the

fire. Various committees were formed to collect relief funds and distribute them, and to arrange housing for those who had been burned out. The city began rebuilding.

The whole United States was building. There had been almost a decade of emigration across the plains now, and the discovery of gold in California made it certain that the already sizeable population on the West Coast was about to mushroom. Transportation was needed, and the Courthouse was the setting for a number of meetings held to promote railroad building. St. Louis, with its western orientation, began promoting a rail line to the West Coast even before it had connections with the east. In 1844 Asa Whitney, a New York businessman, commenced a personal,

The great St. Louis fire, 17 May 1849. The fire, which started on a steamboat and was pushed by an onshore breeze, was punctuated with explosions, both of stored gunpowder and of buildings being blown up for firebreaks. The Old Courthouse, visible at left center, escaped destruction. Lithograph by N. Currier: Courtesy Jefferson National Expansion Memorial

75

nationwide campaign to interest the public in a transcontinental line. In November 1846 he spoke in the
rotunda before an enthusiastic group of local
businessmen. A resolution was passed and sent to
Congress urging adoption of the idea.

The arrival of telegraph lines at the Mississippi in
1847 sparked interest in also establishing rail connections with the East. In December a throng
gathered in the rotunda to discuss the question. The
main result of the meeting was the passage of a resolution calling on the city to subscribe $500,000 towards
extension of the Ohio and Mississippi Railroad line
from Cincinnati to St. Louis. In due time, the money
was provided.

Through the 1850s the building of a transcontinental railroad that would bind the newly acquired
western territories to the eastern half of the country
became one of the nation's prime concerns. It would
be a monumental task. The rails would have to be laid
across seventeen hundred miles of deserts and mountains, and opposition from the Indians was inevitable.
But the project would go forward. A basic decision
had to be made first, though: Which section of the
country, North, South, or Middle, would be the
eastern terminus for the proposed rail line? In October 1849, after several preliminary meetings, a great
railroad convention met in the Courthouse rotunda to
consider the issue. Delegates came from fourteen
states. Senator Benton addressed the assembly, insist-
ing that St. Louis' central position on the Mississippi
made it the logical starting point for the railroad. He
ended his oration with a vivid description of a giant
statue of Columbus that he envisioned carved out of
some mountain overlooking the railroad pass through
the Rockies. The colossus would be "pointing with
outstretched arm to the western horizon, and saying
to the flying passenger, 'There is the East! There is
India!'" The only statue to result was one of the senator himself. After his death it was erected in
LaFayette Park with the last seven words of that most
memorable address carved on its pedestal.

Benton may have been inspired to such oratorical
heights on this occasion by competition with the
renowned Stephen A. Douglas, president of the convention and a representative of Chicago interests.
Friends had asked Senator Benton to attend the meeting and counteract the rising influence of Douglas

who was a leading contender for president of the United States. Benton agreed to attend but declared that, "Douglas can never be president, sir. His legs are too short, sir. His coat, like a cow's tail, hangs too near the ground, sir."

Despite the senator's eloquence and political weight, his central route, utilizing Cochetopa Pass, was never built. It was a mountainous and difficult route; besides, the Civil War eliminated the southern states and Missouri from competition. The first transcontinental rail line, completed in 1869, ran from Chicago and Council Bluffs (Omaha).

The rotunda was host to other railroad meetings. A gathering took place in 1852 to promote a north-south road to supplement Mississippi River traffic.

On 22 April 1857 tracks of the Ohio and Mississippi Railroad finally reached Illinois Town (East St. Louis), linking the Atlantic Ocean with the Mississippi below the Missouri River for the first time. In June a great convention took place to note the event. One thousand distinguished guests were invited. Among them were George Bancroft, the noted historian and diplomat, and the ministers from France, Belgium, and Russia.

Westward expansion and the slavery issue were closely related. Each new addition of western land raised anew the question of whether slavery should be permitted in the new areas. Under the Missouri Compromise of 1820 Missouri was admitted as a slave state, balanced by the admission of free-soil Maine. The dividing line between future free and slave states in the Louisiana Purchase was drawn along Missouri's southern boundary.

The slavery question arose again in 1848 with the acquisition of vast holdings from Mexico. Under the resulting Compromise of 1850, California joined the Union as a free state, while the South gained a stronger fugitive slave law. At the same time, North and South agreed to suspend the slavery issue for the rest of the former Mexican possessions.

Sectional strife became more bitter in 1854 when Senator Stephen Douglas called for the organization of the Kansas and Nebraska territories, part of the Missouri Compromise area, with the slavery question left open to future popular vote. Douglas wished to see the area settled primarily for the benefit of his Chicago-to-San Francisco rail line. The result, however, was "Bleeding Kansas" where civil war raged between southern sympathizers, mostly from Missouri, and "free-soilers," each rushing to populate the territory and gain a majority over the other. The crisis was further heightened by the United States Supreme Court's Dred Scott decision (described later in this book) in 1857, which held that slavery could not be excluded from the new territories regardless of the majority will.

Although open to slavery from the beginning, Missouri was a border state and attracted settlers from both north and south. The Courthouse was open to all. In September 1846 a large gathering of slaveholders met in the rotunda to request measures "for the protection of slave property against the evil

78

When Kansas gained territorial status in 1854 the issue of whether it would be slave or free was left open, which lead to an acrimonious and sometimes bloody national debate. The Old Courthouse was the natural place for St. Louisans to meet, so in August 1856 this meeting took place, which started in the rotunda, but soon spilled outside. From a photo by John H. Fitzgibbon engraved in *Leslie's Illustrated Newspaper*, 13 September 1856: Courtesy Jefferson National Expansion Memorial

designs of abolitionists and others.'' The group passed resolutions calling for after-dark curfews on all Negroes, enforcement of the fugitive slave laws, and prevention of all Negro gatherings for ''teaching'' and ''preaching.'' They also demanded that the county officials enforce the laws governing free Negroes, and appoint a special county patrol.

In August 1856 a larger number of citizens gathered in the rotunda to consider the general situation in Kansas. Both pro- and anti-slavery people attended, but the assemblage was dominated by southern sympathizers who passed resolutions supporting the pro-slavery element in Kansas and calling on the federal government for help. Toward the end of the meeting the crowd grew so large that it had to move outside. A free-soil observer of the proceedings made these comments as reported in *Frank Leslie's Illustrated Newspaper,* 13 September 1856:

I, with many other Free-Soilers, also attended, out of curiosity. I shall not rehearse the cut-and-dried resolutions passed, or rather that the Chairman said were passed. This I doubt; the ''Noes'' were certainly as many as the ''Ayes.'' There were probably about 1,500 present. Great confusion ensued during the progress of the meeting, and very little of the speaking could be heard . . . . And now, our turn is next. We will show some of the 'principal citizens' that St. Louis is a Free-Soil, Anti-slavery city. The merchants, as a body, are utterly opposed to the further extension of the slavery curse. The 45,000 Germans en masse, are opposed to slavery in any shape. The line of demarkation was down this afternoon, and hereafter there are but two parties in this city—Proslavery and Anti-slavery. We are not afraid to speak and act in this matter. We know that three-fourths of our population are utterly opposed to the throat-cutting Missouri Border Ruffians.

The line between free-soilers and pro-slavery people was not drawn so sharply as early as the above writer indicates. Even after several southern states had seceded much sentiment remained in St. Louis for moderation and compromise. This was reflected in a mass meeting held in the east yard of the Courthouse on 12 January 1861. The assembled citizens approved a number of lengthy resolutions calling for support of the Union but condemning the use of military force by either the federal government or the seceding states. Most significantly, the assembly urged a return to the Missouri Compromise line of 1820, a suggestion that was received with great enthusiasm. "Three times three" cheers were given Senator John J. Crittendon, the originator of the proposal. The meeting adjourned, but the crowd demanded a speech from Uriel Wright. The noted orator obliged after which three cheers were given for the Union.

Well before the guns sounded at Fort Sumter, and while moderate citizens still were working for a compromise solution, extreme free-soilers and secessionists were arming and organizing for war. In St. Louis, the "Minutemen," on the side of secession, were encouraged by Claiborne Jackson, the pro-southern governor of Missouri. On the other side were Frank Blair and his German militia.

The Minutemen made their move on 4 March, the day of Lincoln's inauguration. Their plan, according to one account, was to force a confrontation with Blair's sympathizers downtown, and in the ensuing confusion take the federal arsenal in the southern part of the city which, with its sixty thousand muskets, was the key to the entire state. To provoke Blair's forces the Minutemen raised a Confederate flag over their headquarters in the Berthold Mansion at Broadway and Pine, and during the night, a Missouri state flag, then a pro-Confederate symbol, over the dome of the Courthouse. The next morning custodian Quigley promptly hauled down the offending state banner, but the Confederate flag remained. An excited crowd gathered at Minuteman headquarters, but Blair, perhaps suspecting the scheme, restrained his followers.

May 10 was the day of reckoning. Governor Jackson had consolidated his Minutemen, along with other supporters, into the legally constituted state guard that on 6 May went into bivouac at Camp Jackson (named for the governor) east of Grand Avenue, between Olive and Laclede. On 10 May Frank Blair's German regiments and a small force of regulars, all under command of Captain Lyon of the Regular Army, neatly surrounded and disarmed the pro-Confederate militia. Although there would be more fighting in the state, with this act St. Louis, and ultimately the state, were secured for the Union.

In the tense days of
maneuvering just before the
Civil War it was not at all
clear which way St. Louis and
Missouri would go, Union or
Confederate. Confederate
sympathizers under Governor

Jackson organized at the
hastily created "Camp
Jackson" (Above), on the
west side of town. But after a
few days of drilling (note
drum corps, right center) they
were surrounded and disarmed

*by German militia and Union
forces. Missouri stayed with
the Union.* Courtesy Missouri
Historical Society

Future meetings at the Courthouse would be held to further the war effort against the Confederacy. However Uriel Wright, who so often had shaken the rotunda with his oratory, would never again be heard in St. Louis. Although a Union supporter, Wright was outraged by the Camp Jackson affair. He denounced Lincoln, Blair, and Lyon from the steps of the Planters House Hotel and immediately afterwards left St. Louis to join the Confederate Army.

The war failed to dim the city's chamber of commerce spirit. In June 1862 the Courthouse was host to a throng of citizens gathered to persuade the government to build a proposed navy yard in St. Louis. The usual series of resolutions was passed, and a three-man delegation sent to Washington.

In July 1862 an enthusiastic throng filled the ground floor and galleries of the rotunda and the Fourth Street yard. The purpose of the meeting was to encourage enlistments in a brigade being organized under Frank Blair, now a general of volunteer troops. The principal address was given by General Blair himself. Shortly afterwards, the Board of County Commissioners met and pledged $100,000 for support of the volunteers' families.

In 1864 the Union army's original three-year enlistments began to expire; at the same time, enthusiasm for military glory was not the same as it had been three years earlier. The government's answer to its manpower problem was to put into effect a national conscription act passed the year before. Men who did not care to serve could pay an exemption fee of $300, or flee to Canada, or hire a substitute, usually through a broker, at the current market price. The exemption fee was good only until the next draft call, and fleeing to Canada was both inconvenient and illegal, so hiring a substitute was the most popular choice for those able to pay.

The states and localities, with the aid of bounties, tried to fill their draft quotas with volunteers rather than become involved in the difficulties of administering a law that so openly discriminated against the poor. But despite all efforts, volunteering was not entirely successful in St. Louis. There were at least four substitute brokerage offices in the city in July 1864. In the same month a group of citizens met in the Courthouse to propose measures to improve the substitution system. A steering committee suggested that those wishing replacements might either hire them through an authorized committee for the full amount, agree to pay monthly installments, or make their own arrangements. The following month the county found it necessary to appropriate $400,000 for bounties to induce volunteering. Still St. Louis managed its Civil War recruiting reasonably well, and at least was spared violence. New York had been subjected to a four-day reign of terror by an anti-draft mob the previous year.

There were two further public events worthy of note in the 1860s. On 4 July 1862 the Courthouse was officially declared complete, and the occasion marked with appropriate ceremonies.

In April 1865 news of General Lee's surrender was telegraphed to St. Louis. No sooner had the Courthouse been decorated to celebrate the victory than the city received notice of Lincoln's assassination. Architect Rumbold wove black streamers through the red, white, and blue bunting, and designed for the rotunda a cenotaph or monument to honor the slain president. The cenotaph is described in the *St. Louis Dispatch* of 22 April 1865 as a platform twenty-four feet long, thirty feet wide and three feet high with a canopy supported by eight columns twelve feet high. In the center of the platform was a bust of the president resting on a three foot high "tomb." The whole was decorated in a funereal manner. Six gas lamps, each on a standard twelve feet high, ranged around the circumference to provide illumination. The cenotaph remained for thirty days guarded by a detail of soldiers from the 41st Missouri Regiment. A tribute to the impressiveness of the memorial came from several aged persons who insisted to the National Park Service staff in 1942 that as small children they had seen the body of the martyred president himself.

Toward the end of the century an increasing number of rooms were available in St. Louis for public gatherings, and the Courthouse was used less for this purpose. One of the last and most graphically described occurrences was a reception held for President Grover Cleveland in 1887. The event is detailed in the 5 October issue of the *Globe-Democrat*:

Long before the Presidential party was up, there had gathered quite a crowd around the Lindell Hotel. It was 8 o'clock when the committee, of which Mr. R. P. Tansey was Chairman, put in an appearance and escorted the President to his carriage waiting at the door. He was driven east to Fourth Street, south on Fourth to Chestnut, and entered the Court House at the Chestnut Street door. He was greeted by a large crowd which manifested a desire to crowd in after him and were only kept back by the police. Within the rotunda of the Court House the decorations were very neat and attractive. All around the circle were arranged plants and palms, while the walls were covered with red, white and blue bunting. Electric lights were burning among the shrubbery and the gas jets were lighted. The decorations extended to the third gallery above the ground floor, shrubbery being arranged around the railings and calcium lights shine through. The mural paintings, which by the way, are as fine specimens of that character of work as there are in the country, did not appear to very good advantage, the plaster peeling off in places. The pillars supporting the upper balconies were draped in red, white and blue, and the spaces under the balcony were also covered by the national colors. The stars and stripes appeared everywhere, and the shrubbery gave a very pleasing effect. Right at the entrance to the rotunda a hexagonal pavilion had been erected. The sides of the pavilion were draped with dark green plush curtains, trimmed with old gold, while the main entrance was draped with silk plush curtains in blue and old gold. Within the pavilion was a little table and on the table was a high art pitcher with an enameled glass by its side. A revolving chair completed the furnishing of the pavilion. The President entered the rotunda on the arm of Col. Prather, and Col. John I. Martin took the President's overcoat. He was led to the pavilion and depositing his hat on the table, stood rubbing his hands. "Are you ready?" Col. Prather asked. "Yes, I'm ready." "Let it begin," said the Chief Magistrate of 50,000,000 people, as if he felt like throwing up the position and escaping it. First, a delegation was received from the Western Commercial Travelers' Protective Association, about 200 of the gay drummers passing and grasping the President's hand. They behaved with decorum, and when they had left, the reception took on a miscellaneous aspect. There were laborers in cardigans and overalls, and dudes in the latest habilimental agony. There were old Irish women wearing bonnets and shawls; German women of vast proportions both as to length and breadth, little girls

86

clinging to their skirts. Fashionably dressed women bowed before the President as they grasped his hand. A couple of old Irish women insisted on giving the President both their hands, and then departed making a kind of jerky genuflexion. He shook the hands of several infants in arms, much to the gratification of their mothers. How much feeling there was in his hand-shake was illustrated when Col. Prather handed him a glass of water. He drank from it holding it in his left hand and looking up to the top of the dome while the good right hand went on pumping all the time. For a long hour and a half he stood the siege (9 a.m. to 10:30). When the door was closed, he heaved a sigh of relief and went to his carriage. He reached the Southern Hotel where Mrs. Cleveland and Mrs. Francis entered the carriage with Mayor Francis. They were driven to the Levee at the foot of Chestnut Street to take the boat for the excursion down the river.

Reception for President Cleveland in the Old Courthouse. From the *Missouri Republican,* 5 October 1887. Courtesy Jefferson National Expansion Memorial

87

The Spanish governors who ruled the Louisiana Territory before American acquisition had absolute authority in legal matters. Neither juries nor lawyers were necessary parts of the system, nor did the governors always bother to advise the people of the decrees and ordinances they lived under until judgment had been passed.

Nevertheless, the inhabitants of St. Louis regretted Spain's departure, for her governors had been popular rulers, and on the whole their justice had been fair, swift, and had cost little or nothing. On the other hand, the theoretically more humane and democratic American system of justice was one of the most tedious and expensive on earth. When the territory came under United States administration, trade was temporarily halted due to the delay and expense of instituting the new legal system.

If, under the American legal system, lawyers prolonged the duration and inflated the cost of litigation, they also provided their fellow citizens with a good deal of entertainment by their courtroom oratory. Many of the noted speakers of the last century who sent thrills around the rotunda with their words were also lawyers who drew capacity crowds of spectators to hear them "plead," as it was called, in the courtrooms.

In 1849 a visiting Scotsman described a trial then in progress. The youth of the judge, and the fact that he did not wear a gown, struck the visitor as a defect, but he remained the entire day, spellbound by the oratory of the defense counsel:

A plain, middle-sized man, about thirty years of age, had charge of the prisoner's defense (it was some shooting charge). He began in slow, rather feeble accents, and, as I thought, far from the main question. He seemed to rise mentally, however, and even in person. He spoke fluently, pertinently, and with grace and ease for at least two hours. The scene deepened; his voice became more sonorous; his whole soul seemed thrown into the case of his client. I shall never again doubt of magnetism. I was perfectly spellbound. I felt no weariness, nor hunger; no thirst, nor inconvenience of any kind, though I had to stand in a crowded courtroom the whole day. For six hours did this tide of perfectly tremendous eloquence roll along, and still it seemed to be gathering power. I have never

90

heard anything that could be compared to the elo-
quence of this gifted orator. I said in my heart, the
court that has counsel like this requires no other orna-
ment. I have heard Jeffreys, Campbell and Brougham,
but never heard anything like this. I inquired his
name; I think they told me that it was Wright.

This was Uriel Wright, mentioned before in connection with the Courthouse.

At one time or another nearly every type of state
and local court was quartered in the building. The
federal courts were here only briefly. When the
Courthouse first opened for business in 1843, the
U.S. Circuit Judge was allowed use of the lower west
room when not needed by the county. By 1854, the
U.S. Court had found rented quarters in the Papin
Building located on Main Street between Pine and
Chestnut.

The city's busiest court, in terms of the number of
cases processed, was never in the Courthouse despite
attempts to locate here. This was the recorder's court,
the municipal tribunal charged with trying minor offenses. The early newspapers devoted a generous
amount of space to relate the amusing antics of the
drunks, disorderlies, and painted ladies who passed
before the recorder.

In 1845 the city, not having adequate space of its
own, petitioned the county for one of the rooms in the
east wing of the building for the recorder's court, and
for basement space in the new west wing for use as a
jail. The judges of the county court refused the request, stating that the rooms were needed for county
purposes and besides, they did not wish to fill the
Courthouse with the class of people usually brought
before the city recorder!

Fourteen years later the city still was trying to find
a place for its recorder's court. In 1859 Mayor O. D.
Filley explained that the present courtroom stank hor-
ribly, especially on Mondays when business was at its
peak, and that he thought one of the rooms in the
north wing of the Courthouse, then under construction, would make a fine place for the recorder's court.
The mayor's request was denied. The county officials
were willing to turn the entire north wing over to the
city for use as a city hall but they were still determined
to exclude the lower classes of wrongdoers and their
bad smells from the elegant new palace of justice.

In 1860 or 1861, the recorder's court found lodging on the second floor of the firehouse on Seventh, between Pine and Olive streets. At this place in June of the latter year the unlucky court received a volley of musket fire from a nervous company of home guards who thought they were being sniped at from the balcony of the court by Confederate sympathizers. Six people were killed and others wounded.

The county did permit an additional city function which caused some minor problems. In 1864 the assessor complained that acid was leaking into his office from the batteries of the fire alarm telegraph in the room above. In 1866 the records reveal that the same telegraph was causing "certain nuisances" on the roof of the north wing. In 1868 the telegraph was again in trouble. The superintendent of the device asked the court if he might run a pipe from his battery room to the ladies' privy beneath, apparently to drain off the still offending acid. The county ruled favorably on his request.

The city gained exclusive jurisdiction over the Courthouse in March 1877, after St. Louis City and County were divorced by the state legislature. By this time, the recorder's court (now known as the police court), jail, city hall, and fire alarm telegraph had found quarters in other public buildings completed in the early 1870s. After separation, the Courthouse continued to serve the city as it had the county.

The Courthouse was at its busiest between its completion date in 1862 and its delivery to the city in 1877. During this period it housed, among other things, the court of criminal corrections, the circuit court, the criminal court, the State Supreme Court, the probate court, the court of common pleas, the land court, and the law commissioner's court. In 1865 the latter three tribunals were absorbed into the circuit court, but at the same time the court of criminal corrections, which had overlapping jurisdiction with the city police court, was created.

If all this seems confusing to a layman, it also bewildered lawyers and judges. In 1867 Julia Higgins, the proprietress of a bawdy house, was arrested and fined $50 by the police court. The very next day the unfortunate business woman was arrested again for the same offense and this time brought before the court of criminal corrections which fined her $100! The St. Louis *Missouri Republican* in its issue for 12 December 1867 reports that this was only the latest in a series of such incidents. The collection of revenue from these establishments was put on a more orderly basis when they were legalized under a new city charter in 1870.

Human nature has not significantly changed since 1843, and the law has remained one of society's more conservative institutions. Accordingly, the questions argued in the building, and the manner in which they were handled, generally did not differ greatly from the issues and procedures occupying the courts today.

In his memoirs, *Notes Taken in Sixty Years*, lawyer Richard S. Elliott has left us an interesting account of a trial held in 1847 in which he was a defense counsel. The case was heard in the criminal court which was then on the first floor of the original courthouse, torn down in 1851 to make way for the present east wing. Elliott, along with Uriel Wright, was engaged to defend a man charged with striking his mother-in-law over the head with a length of oaken clapboard. In his memoirs Elliott states that mother-in-law jokes were not yet popular, and consequently, the defense was not so easy as it would have been in later years.

The defendant's in-laws, not content with the circuit attorney, hired Thomas Hudson to prosecute the case. Elliot believed his client guilty and decided he could win only by avoiding the merits of the case and somehow undermining the prosecutor's presentation to the jury.

An incident involving prosecution lawyer Hudson at Fort Leavenworth early in the Mexican War, then just recently passed, gave the defense its opportunity. Captain Hudson, at the head of his newly recruited Laclede Rangers, had reached the fort in the evening. Due to army red tape, the company could not be fed until the next morning. The only thing Hudson had to pacify his angry men with was a dose of oratory: "Yes, we shall knock at the gates of Santa Fe, as Ethan Allen knocked at the gates of Ticonderoga, and to the question—Who's there? We shall reply—open these gates in the name of the Great Jehovah and the Laclede Rangers! . . . But suppose . . . the fellows inside should call out—are you the same Laclede Rangers who went whining around Fort Leavenworth in search of a supper?" Elliott related the story to the jury in a humorous manner, suggesting that Captain

Richard Smith Elliott, prominent St. Louis lawyer of the mid-19th century. Elliott often practiced in the Old Courthouse and his book, Notes Taken in Sixty Years *(R. P. Studley, St. Louis, 1883), is a valuable window on the period.* Artotype by R. Benecke: Courtesy Jefferson National Expansion Memorial

Hudson's speech to them was no more a substitute for the truth than his oration at Fort Leavenworth had been proper substitute for his men's supper.

Elliott won the case with the help of Wright, who by his verbal slight of hand, transformed the club into an insignificant stick. Instead of being pleased with himself, however, Elliott felt uneasy for having helped acquit an obviously guilty man. "I began to feel like an accessory after the fact. It is a pretty theory, that everybody charged with crime shall have a fair trial; but I began to ask myself the question whether the trial ought not to be fair to the State as well as to the defendant? . . . I was clearly on the side of the criminal classes and acting against society!"

Elliott practiced law for two more years, then became a successful St. Louis real estate operator and businessman.

In 1851 Prince William of Prussia, later Emperor of Germany, brought suit to recover $7,000 of Prussian government funds. He claimed the money had been embezzled by Herr Knepper, formerly postmaster at Vermelkirchen, who had fled from his homeland to the United States after the failure of the 1848 revolution.

Charles Gibson, retained by the emperor to represent him, filed a claim in the St. Louis circuit court against the estate of Knepper who had since died. The court ruled that it did not have authority to accept litigation submitted by a foreign sovereign. The state supreme court decided otherwise and returned the case to a lower court. For winning this important point of international law, Gibson received from Prince William two magnificent four-foot high porcelain vases made by the royal potteries. The vases now are on display in the south wing of the Courthouse. They rest in the same niches which are seen in the photograph of the 1845 structure (p. 30).

One of the more notorious cases tried in the Courthouse involved Henry Shaw, creator of the Missouri Botanical Garden and Tower Grove Park. Shaw amassed a fortune in the hardware business and at the age of forty retired to enjoy his wealth. There was another who also wished to enjoy Shaw's wealth. In 1859, when fifty-nine years old, he was sued for breach of promise by Miss Effie Carstang. The plaintiff's lawyer was Uriel Wright. The great orator must have outdone himself on this occasion. He succeeded in convincing the jury that Miss Carstang had been

94

One of the vases presented to Charles Gibson by Emperor William I of Prussia, for winning an important case. The niches in the south ground floor hallway, where the vases now are displayed, were once on the outside wall of the building; they are visible in the photograph on p. 30. Photos by Joseph Matthews: Courtesy Jefferson National Expansion Memorial

Previous page: *The sensational 1880 breach-of-promise trial of Henry Shaw in the second floor courtroom, west wing.* Drawing by G. C. Friedlein in *Harper's Weekly,* 31 March 1860. Courtesy Jefferson National Expansion Memorial

injured to the tune of $100,000. Cooler heads later prevailed and the verdict was reversed. The only real winners were Shaw's lawyers who were said to have become $20,000 richer as a result of the litigation. The trial was held in the oval courtroom on the second floor, west wing, then the court of common pleas.

With the outbreak of the Civil War, the military authorities had enough of their own problems and wished the civil courts to operate as normally as possible. The courts, however, were confused about their wartime role, as shown by the following order issued by General Halleck:

Information having been received that certain judicial officers intrusted with the administration of the criminal laws and ordinances in this department have misunderstood the objects and purposes of the establishment of martial law in this city of St. Louis and in consequence of such misunderstanding have failed to enforce all those laws and ordinances, and as crimes and misdemeanors should at all times be strictly suppressed, it is hereby enjoined upon all such civil officers, whether as judges, attorneys, sheriffs, marshals, coroners, clerks, justices of the peace, presiding officers of police courts, constables, or members of the police to strictly enforce all criminal laws and ordinances; to have arrested, tried and punished in the courts established in the State, and in the manner prescribed by the laws of the State, all persons guilty of any violation of such laws and ordinances, in the same manner as if martial law had not been declared to exist.

After the Civil War radical anti-southern politicians gained control of Missouri and proceeded to pass measures punishing former disloyalty. Their instrument was the Drake test oath. Anyone who wished to hold any kind of public office, or to teach, preach, practice law, or simply vote was required to swear that he had, in no way, at any time, supported or sympathized with the Confederacy. The oath was sweeping and rigid. Since it denied the principle of reconciliation, it was bitterly opposed by Unionists as well as by former Confederate supporters.

The radicals' first act was to remove all public officeholders who refused to accept the oath, particularly from the judiciary. On 14 June 1865 a squad of police under state militia General David C. Coleman marched into the supreme court room in the south wing, second floor of the Courthouse and demanded that the justices hand over all court records and vacate the room. At the same time there were over six hundred soldiers stationed outside the building to prevent any disturbances. On refusing the order, the judges were removed by the police and taken before the recorder where they were charged with disturbing the peace. Three days later a large crowd gathered in the Courthouse yard to protest the ouster.

Frank Blair could never be accused of secessionist sympathies, but he was outraged both by the oath and by the radicals' actions. He put on his major general's uniform, marched to the polls, and demanded to be registered without taking the oath. On refusal, he brought suit against the election officials. The Missouri courts, controlled by the radicals, routinely dismissed all such suits. However the oath eventually was declared unconstitutional by the U.S. Supreme Court, and in 1870 moderate Republicans won firm control of the state government.

The great beer-jerker controversy came in 1867. The question was whether or not to outlaw female waitresses in beer halls. The prosecution painted a frightening picture of the moral abyss that yawned at the feet of innocent young men who might enter these establishments. The defense described the charming romantic scene that existed in Europe. There, from Italy's vine-clad hills to the icy peaks of the North, lady beer servers were a valued part of time honored tradition. The court decided that St. Louis was not Europe, and the beer-jerking menace was ruthlessly suppressed.

An early civil rights case was tried in the Courthouse. In 1866 Mrs. Virginia Louise Minor founded the women's suffrage movement in Missouri. The Woman Suffrage Association of Missouri which grew from this was the first organization in the world to make the enfranchisement of women its sole purpose. In 1872 Mrs. Minor demanded the right to register as a voter. The registrar refused and Mrs. Minor filed suit in the circuit court, in association with her husband, Francis Minor, since at that time women could not sue independently. The local court, the state supreme court, and the U.S. Supreme Court each decided against her. The supreme tribunal

Upper: *Frank Blair, who perhaps more than anyone saved Missouri for the Union, but who was outraged by various "loyalty" acts enacted afterward.* Courtesy Missouri Historical Society

Lower: *Virginia Minor, an early advocate of women's suffrage. Her case was heard in the Old Courthouse. She lost, but the times were changing.* From *History of Woman Suffrage* (Source Book Press, N.Y.) Courtesy Source Book Press

The bronze bust of Louis D. Brandeis from the west courtroom, second floor, where the future Supreme Court Justice was admitted to the bar. Photo by Joseph Matthews: Courtesy Jefferson National Expansion Memorial

unanimously declared, "If the courts can consider any question settled, this is one . . . the Constitution does not confer the right of suffrage on anyone."

There were other Courthouse events that perhaps seemed routine at the time, but involved persons who would become famous later. In 1859 Ulysses S. Grant applied for the position of county engineer. His West Point training well qualified him for the job, but due to political considerations he lost out to another applicant. And in November 1878, Louis D. Brandeis, who eventually would become one of the great justices of the U.S. Supreme Court, was formally admitted to the Bar in circuit court room number four. This is the second floor oval courtroom in the west wing of the building, where a bust of the renowned jurist now stands.

The Courthouse association with slavery has often been exaggerated. Slave auctions from the building's steps were not uncommon and being public they attracted much attention. However, the Courthouse sales, which usually were in connection with the settlement of estates, were insignificant compared to those held elsewhere by commercial dealers. In one issue of a local newspaper, three commercial dealers advertised for five hundred, one thousand, and twenty-five hundred slaves respectively.

In the 1930s the building had a black janitor who for a fee took visitors to the "slave dungeons" in the basement of the east wing. There is a room with barred doors in this part of the building which superficially resembles a jail cell, but it served another purpose. In 1866 the Missouri Historical Society had its first museum here, and at other times court records were kept in the room. The bars were simply to protect the material and at the same time permit circulation of air, which helped prevent stored materials from becoming moldy.

Since the federal courts were in the building for only a short time any federal cases involving slaves, such as violations of the fugitive slave laws, would have been few. Also, most minor offenses concerning slaves were dealt with by the recorder's court which was never in the Courthouse.

Most slavery litigation in the building was heard in the probate and circuit courts. Slaves were sold from the Courthouse steps by order of the courts to satisfy claims against estates or individuals. A slave might

Above: *The last slave sale on the east steps of the Old Courthouse. These sales were estate settlements, not commerical sales.* Painting by Noble: Courtesy Missouri Historical Society

Left: *The iron doors in the basement for many years were thought to have been to slave quarters, but they were simply to provide security with ventilation for various historical records.* Photo by Joseph Matthews: Courtesy Jefferson National Expansion Memorial

also be auctioned for hire while awaiting final disposition of his case. In addition, some Blacks were auctioned off as unclaimed fugitive slaves. If the courts felt it necessary to have a slave locked up, he was lodged in the nearby county jail located at Sixth and Chestnut streets.

Auctions usually were held on the east steps. While the east wing was being rebuilt between 1851 and 1856, sales were held at the south or north doors. The only presently existing structure that can be associated with slave sales is the east portico.

Opposition to slavery increased in St. Louis as the Civil War approached. On 1 January 1861 a slave auction at the Courthouse was disrupted by a jeering mob of two thousand. Nevertheless, slavery remained legal in Missouri until abolished in 1865 by an edict of the governor, and the court records show that slave sales continued to be held at the Courthouse during the war.

Slaves were only one type of property sold at the Courthouse. A variety of other things, under court order or by private individuals, was also auctioned from the steps. One of the most commonly sold items was land. In 1846 Henry Clay tried to sell some of his locally owned acreage from the east portico, but became discouraged, complaining that the large crowd had come only to see him and not to buy his land.

In 1878 Joseph Pulitzer bought the bankrupt *Dispatch* at public auction from the east steps; merged with the *Post* it became the St. Louis *Post-Dispatch*, one of the nation's great newspapers.

Private auctions undoubtedly created problems for the Courthouse authorities and were discouraged as much as possible. The county court records for January 1850 give a hint of this: "The Presiding Justice is requested to call on the Mayor of the City and request him to take necessary means to abate the nuisance of Auction Sales of horses and articles of furniture at the East front of the Courthouse, and all other sales except such legally directed to be made there."

A large number of slaves were freed in the circuit court by their owners. Both Frank Blair and Ulysses S. Grant set free their only slaves here in 1859.

Slaves could also sue for their own freedom. While such litigation was in process, the alleged owner could not remove the Negro from the court's jurisdiction or punish him for bringing suit. Sometimes a slave sued on the grounds that he had been freed by a previous owner's will. Others gained their liberty because their masters had taken them to free territory and then returned to Missouri. The courts commonly granted freedom in these latter cases, until this precedent was reversed by the Dred Scott case.

The Dred Scott case was not newsworthy while it was in this building. It began to arouse interest only after it had moved into the higher courts. Its significance lay in the U.S. Supreme Court decision rendered eleven years later.

Dred Scott was brought to St. Louis from Virginia in 1830 by his master, Peter Blow. Later the Blow family sold Scott to Dr. John Emerson, an army surgeon. The slave accompanied his new owner on tours of duty at Rock Island, Illinois, and Fort Snelling in what is now Minnesota. At the latter place Scott married a slave girl named Harriet, purchased by Dr. Emerson from a fellow officer. In 1843 Emerson died, leaving the Scotts to his widow. In November 1846 Dred and Harriet filed suit against Mrs. Irene Emerson for their freedom on grounds of previous residence in free territory.

As illiterate, pennyless slaves, the Scotts obviously needed help in initiating their suit. The records show that Taylor Blow, the son of Dred's old master, and Joseph Charless, Jr., Blow's brother-in-law, signed bonds for the Scotts when the suit was first filed. Two noted anti-slavery lawyers were involved in the original litigation. One was T. B. Murdock, who had taken such cases before and been criticized by colleagues for his efforts. The other was Charles Drake, father of the Drake test oath.

The case came to trial in June 1847 in the circuit court. The Scotts lost but appealed and won a new trial which began in 1850 in the same court.

The Scotts had been a financial burden rather than an asset to Mrs. Emerson from the beginning, and she probably would not have contested their complaint had it not been for the threat of monetary claims against her. In the second round of litigation, Scott had new lawyers, Alexander P. Field and his partner David N. Hall, who did indeed claim damages amounting to $9,000. The defendant would surely have been glad to forget the whole thing at this point

Dred and Harriet Scott, central figures in one of the most important trials ever held in the Old Courthouse. Photographs by Fitzgibbon, engraved for *Leslie's Illustrated Newspaper,* 27 June 1857

had it not been for the damages asked; in 1849 or early 1850 she had moved to Massachusetts and married Dr. C. C. Chafee, an ardent abolitionist politician. In 1853, in order to save her new husband embarrassment, ownership of the slaves, at least in appearance, was transferred to her brother, John Sanford of New York. The Scotts remained in St. Louis in custody of the court.

The Scotts won the second trial, but the case was appealed to the Missouri State Supreme Court, which in 1852 returned the couple to slavery.

Until then the case was not unusual and had no political overtones; but the majority opinion of the state high court, represented by two of the three justices, clearly reflected the increasing tensions between North and South: "Times now are not as they were when former decisions of this subject were made. Since then not only individuals but states have been possessed with a dark and fell spirit in relation to slavery, whose gratification is sought in the pursuit of measures, whose inevitable consequence must be the overthrow and destruction of our government."

The first two trials were held in the lower west courtroom. The state supreme court was in St. Louis when it considered the case, but it probably did not meet in the Courthouse, since the east wing was being rebuilt which left only two courtrooms available for use.

After the state supreme court decision, the Dred and Harriet Scott case began to attract national attention and the interest of prominent lawyers. Roswell Field (no relation to Alexander), the father of poet Eugene Field, now entered the case and carried litigation for the Scotts to the federal district court, probably meeting in the nearby Papin Building. In May 1854 that court ruled in favor of Sanford. Field immediately appealed to the U. S. Supreme Court.

Much had happened since Dred and Harriet Scott had first applied for their freedom in 1846. A new fugitive slave law had passed in 1850. The Kansas-Nebraska Act of 1854 had repealed the Missouri Compromise, permitting slavery in previously free territory. Pro- and anti-slavery guerrillas were making "Bleeding Kansas" ever more bloodier. Violence even broke forth on the floor of the U.S. Senate when abolitionist senator Charles Sumner was caned nearly to death by South Carolina congressman Preston Brooks.

106

The nation now focused its attention on the U.S. Supreme Court. Some of the country's top legal talent entered the case. Field called to his side Montgomery Blair, brother of Frank Blair and later a member of Lincoln's cabinet. For the defense was Henry S. Geyer, one of the ablest lawyers in the West and the successor to Thomas Hart Benton in the Senate. With him was Reverdy Johnson, a former attorney general of the United States. During the first trial Mrs. Emerson had been represented by G.W. Goode. From the second trial until the appeal to the U.S. Supreme Court the defense was handled by the St. Louis firm of Garland and Norris.

The U.S. Supreme Court heard the case argued twice, once in February of 1856 and again in December. The long awaited verdict was finally delivered on 6 March 1857. The nation's supreme tribunal ruled against the Scotts seven to two. Chief Justice Roger B. Taney read the "opinion of the Court."

In essence, Taney declared that Negroes could not be citizens under the Constitution, and that slave owners could not be deprived of their property or prevented from introducing slavery into the recently acquired western territories. The effect of the decision was to strike a legal death blow at the delicately built framework of compromise that had kept North and South from one another's throats. Taney had hoped to settle the issue of the expansion of slavery and establish lasting peace between the sections for all time; but instead of casting water on the spreading flames of civil strife he had thrown gasoline.

In 1857 the chief justice was the most popular man in the South and the most hated in the North. Among the milder epithets, he was called a "traitor to the Constitution" and a "spotted mush toad." A description attributed to Lincoln declared that his decision was "as thin as homeopathic soup made by boiling the shadow of a pigeon that had starved to death."

Although Taney was a southerner and wished to protect the South from the growing political strength of the North, he was not the totally depraved monster that he seemed to be at the time. His remark that the Negro "had no rights which the white man was bound to respect," was seized upon with glee by his enemies. He had meant the words as a statement of the legal consensus that existed at the time the Constitution was written, and they did not necessarily reflect his

Upper: *Roger B. Taney, Chief Justice of the U.S. Supreme Court in 1857 during the Dred Scott trials.* Courtesy National Archives

Lower: *Judge William M. Kinsey on the bench in the "Dred Scott Room," the lower west wing courtroom. This photo was taken in 1904, after the courtroom actually used for the Dred Scott case had been remodeled into two smaller courtrooms.* Courtesy Jefferson National Expansion Memorial

108

personal feelings. Taney had freed his own slaves and purchased others so that they might work out their freedom. The chief justice's greatest blunder was in supposing his decision could halt the nation's slide into civil war. The decision only hastened it.

Dred Scott became famous during the extended litigation. His portrait was painted and can now be seen at the Missouri Historical Society. After the decision, ownership of Dred and Harriet Scott was transferred to Taylor Blow, who then freed the family. The Scotts made their last appearance in the Courthouse to register as free negroes:

May 4, 1858. Dred Scott aged fifty years, five feet four inches high, and by occupation a porter; and Harriett Scott aged forty years, five feet four inches high and by occupation a washerwoman came into Court and severally proved to the satisfaction of the Court that they are of the Class of free negroes who may be licensed to remain in this state, that they are of good character and behavior, and capable of supporting themselves by honest employment; and moreover having entered into bonds in the penal sums of One Thousand Dollars each conditioned according to law, with Taylor Blow as security, which bonds are approved by the Court, it is therefore ordered that the said Dred Scott and Harriett Scott be severally licensed to remain in the State during good behavior.

After fighting his case for eleven years, Scott enjoyed only fifteen months of freedom. In September 1858 he died of tuberculosis.

As the first major presence of the U.S. justice system west of the Mississippi, the Old Courthouse saw cases that ranged from the trivial and even humorous, to those that affected the destiny of the nation and millions of lives. It waded through the dry technicalities of corporate law, and experienced the more dramatic pathos and joy of human beings encountering the law at some turning point. Ironically, the legal story of the building ended where it began, with the Chouteaus and Lucases. The heirs of these illustrious pioneers attempted to regain possession of the courthouse square after the courts vacated it, on the grounds that the land no longer served its intended purpose. The case went to the state supreme court, which ruled against the plaintiffs in December 1932.

Upper: *During the Depression and after the courts had moved to new quarters various organizations used the decaying building, including the St. Louis Art League. (This room is in the upper east wing: it is now the publications office where this book was produced.)* Courtesy Jefferson National Expansion Memorial

Lower: *Roof rehabilitation undertaken in 1978.* Photo by Joseph Bilello: Courtesy Jefferson National Expansion Memorial

110

The Old Courthouse had seen incredible changes in the territory it served. The building that had been a gathering point for pioneers planning their trek across empty plains remained to be deeply involved in the amazing development of the West (and saw its caseload grow accordingly), and finally began to see a time of troubles as joblessness grew in the densely populated land. Finally the work outgrew the structure. In 1930 the courts moved to larger, modern quarters in the new skyscraper Civil Courts Building at Twelfth and Market streets, although three rooms continued to be used by justices of the peace and their constables. The remaining space was used in many ways. These were the Depression years, and several volunteer social service groups as well as the local Works Progress Administration headquarters were based in the Old Courthouse. (The venerable building had acquired the "Old" in her name now, and wore it proudly.) A museum of science and industry occupied some of the rooms. The St. Louis Art League held meetings and displayed paintings in the rotunda, and did much to preserve interest in the building after the courts left, along with a program of historic markers and publicity by the Junior Chamber of Commerce. But without a single, active administering body the building was not well-maintained, and there was deterioration. In 1936 a fire, probably caused by faulty wiring, broke out in the attic of the west wing. The flames destroyed the ceiling of the large oval courtroom, and the heat damaged Wimar's painting of Cochetopa Pass. A wooden beam charred by the fire still can be seen in the north wing.

Restoration work in the upper courtroom, west wing.
Courtesy Jefferson National Expansion Memorial

St. Louis was aware of the architectural and historical significance of the building, and in 1940 deeded it to the federal government for preservation. The National Park Service began preservation by rebuilding the roofs of all four wings, as they had begun to deteriorate badly. The wrought iron framework and copper covering of the 1850s and 1860s was replaced with new steel frames covered with lead-coated copper. On the dome new copper plates were placed directly over the original copper of 1861. The roof was rehabilitated again in 1978.

The restoration of the building has required first a major effort to discover the history of its construction. This has not been so easy as one might expect. Early plans or sketches are rare since blueprints, with

Restoration work on the
cupola and flagpole, 1979.
Gateway Arch in background.
Photo by Joseph Matthews:
Courtesy Jefferson National
Expansion Memorial

multiple copies, were not developed until after this building was basically done, so early plans were hand-drawn, often with no copies. (When William Twombly replaced Henry Singleton as architect in 1842, one of his first jobs was to re-draw the plans. Apparently Singleton's set had just worn out from use during early construction.) Although the last major remodeling of the building's interior occurred in the rotunda in 1870 and the west wing in 1885, there have been many minor alterations since those dates. Many of these changes were made between 1894 and 1914 when stairways, partitions, doors, windows, and courtroom furnishings were eliminated, added, or rebuilt. Those portions of the building now being used as National Park Service offices occasionally see such internal modifications. In the public areas, the oval courtroom on the second floor of the west wing is the only major section of the building's interior other than the rotunda to survive essentially intact, though its ceiling was replaced after the 1936 fire. Through restoration the second floor east courtroom now looks as it did when first completed in 1856, although the fixed furnishings date from the first decade of this century. Several smaller features remain. The louvered, wooden shutters presently in the lobby are believed to have been installed about 1856 when the east wing was first completed. The arch-shaped niches in the alcoves of the south wing are part of the 1845 structure. The fountain and iron fence of the 1860s were removed about 1890, but reproductions have been installed since. (The column capitals in the northeast and northwest yards are not from the Old Courthouse. They were saved from buildings that were demolished to create the park for Gateway Arch, and moved here for public display.)

National Park Service painting restoration specialist Walter Nitkiewicz at work, 1978.
Courtesy Jefferson National Expansion Memorial

One of the final steps in the restoration of the Old Courthouse has been the treatment of the interior decorations of the rotunda. These have been a difficult problem, both to ascertain just who did what, and to decide how to restore and maintain them. In 1955 National Park Service restoration and preservation specialists under the direction of Walter Nitkiewicz began a close examination of the whole scheme, and more research was accomplished in 1978. They carefully removed patches of paint and plaster, noting the paint layers, the types of paint, and the painting styles. At the same time other people,

The extensive study of the rotunda decorations undertaken in 1978-79 required scaffolding the entire height of the rotunda. One of many things discovered was an unexpected design of stars in the dome panels, long ago painted over. This star was found above the figure of "Law" (see p. 58). Photo by Joseph Matthews: Courtesy Jefferson National Expansion Memorial

114

notably Lincoln B. Spiess of St. Louis, were examining historical documents for whatever they could reveal. To sum up a complex and still-not-completely-resolved situation, it appears that, with the exception of the lunettes, all the presently visible decorations are the work of Ettore Miragoli. (As mentioned earlier, the paintings in the small upper dome are exact copies of Miragoli paintings that were not salvageable.) The intervening surfaces in plain color are National Park Service work from the early 1940s, done under the direction of John Bryan. The lunettes, originally by Wimar and therefore of great artistic interest, had been worked on by several different artists between 1862 and 1921. Besides these many hands, time, dirt and weather (and the heat of the 1936 west courtroom fire in the case of the west lunette) had done their work. Walter Nitkiewicz and his staff accomplished what could be done in cleaning the paintings, fastening down loose paint, and in cases where it was feasible, revealing earlier details. The paintings do appear to still follow Wimar's composition, but the execution is almost all that of later, less talented hands.

The building now is a part of Jefferson National Expansion Memorial, a unit of the National Park Service that commemorates the westward expansion of the United States. The exterior is to be maintained as it appeared in the 1870s. Inside is a museum of St. Louis' role in the westward movement of the American people. The old, worn limestone slabs in the rotunda that have seen so much history now echo to thousands of footsteps as visitors browse and look at the exhibits, or the murals. Many a St. Louis grade-schooler has gotten his first real "touch" of western history as a National Park Service ranger has shown him the spots where it happened. The building is still a St. Louis meeting place. Often the casual visitor discovers a concert, or lecture, or some public celebration taking place in the venerable old building. The builders built well.

Rally during the presidential campaign, 1976. Photo by Joseph Matthews: Courtesy Jefferson National Expansion Memorial

Appendix

Chronology

1826
*First Courthouse built on this site, which formerly
was part of St. Louis' "common field" at the west
edge of town.*

1839
*First Courthouse hopelessly outgrown by the city's
rapid growth: after a design contest work begins on
Henry Singleton's plan of a new Courthouse,
which incorporates the first Courthouse as one of
its four wings. Cornerstone laid 21 October.*

1842
*First office of present building occupied in April;
construction still proceeding.*

1845
*First stage of construction essentially complete, the
original Courthouse, its cupola removed, still
forming the east wing. The dome much smaller
than the present one.*

1847
*First of the Dred Scott trials; decision goes
against Scott.*

1849
*National Railroad Convention held in Courthouse;
Senator Benton makes famous "There lies the
East" speech. Great St. Louis Fire, but Courthouse
escapes damage. Mass meetings in the Courthouse
to deal with the Great Fire and the cholera
emergency.*

1850
*Second Dred Scott trial held in building; Scott
wins, but case appealed, eventually to reach the
U.S. Supreme Court.*

1851
*First Courthouse, acting until now as the east wing
of the large Courthouse, torn down.*

1852
New east wing started.

1853

New south wing started. Gas lighting installed

1856

East wing completed; north wing begun.

1859

Designs submitted for a new, larger dome.
Controversy erupts whether William Rumbold's
design for a wrought and cast iron dome is strong
enough, resulting in testing of a scale model. His
design is chosen.

1860

West and south wings complete. Construction
begins on new dome.

1861

Construction of large wrought and cast iron dome
complete.

1862

Murals and decorations added to interior of dome;
Carl Wimar does lunnetes and portraits.
Courthouse construction declared complete; total
cost $1,199,871.

1869

Spiral staircase removed from center of rotunda.

1880

Ettore Miragoli redecorates dome interior.

1887

August Becker retouches Wimar paintings.

1905

Prof. Edmund Wuerpel restores Wimar paintings.

1921

James Lyons retouches Wimar paintings.

1930

Use of building as Courthouse ends. Courts move
to new Federal Building at 12th and Market.
During Depression years various public uses of
building, including art classes and displays.

1935
Jefferson National Expansion Memorial (which eventually includes the Old Courthouse and Gateway Arch) created by President Franklin D. Roosevelt.

1936
Fire in the dome, probably from faulty wiring, damages murals.

1940
Federal government receives title to the building from City of St. Louis. New roof installed, interior restoration begins.

1941
Jefferson National Expansion Memorial puts offices in Old Courthouse; museum exhibits installed.

1942
Restoration considered complete.

1955
More restoration undertaken, including research and repair on interior decorations.

1979
Work underway on roof rehabilitation, mural restoration, and new museum exhibit plan.

Development of the Old Courthouse
1826-1864

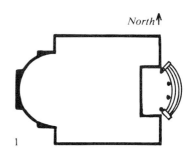

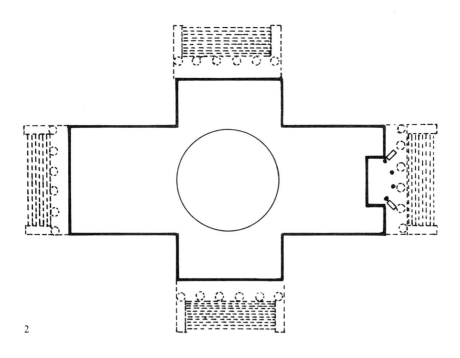

(1) *Brick Courthouse, built 1826-1828. Demolished 1851-1852. Laveille and Morton, architects.*

(2) *Courthouse built 1839-1845 and as it existed until 1852, the brick courthouse serving as the east wing. General plan by Henry Singleton: dotted lines indicate portions planned but not built.*

(3) *Courthouse as completed 1852-1864 under Robert Mitchell and William Rumbold.*

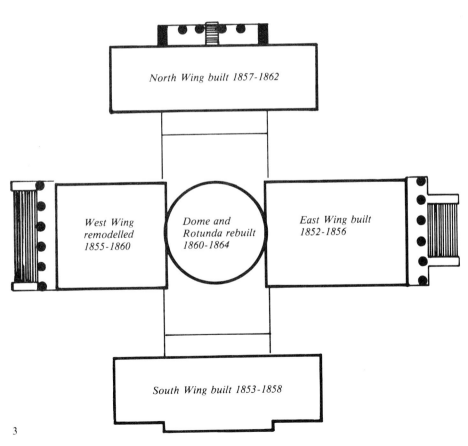

North Wing built 1857-1862

West Wing remodelled 1855-1860

Dome and Rotunda rebuilt 1860-1864

East Wing built 1852-1856

South Wing built 1853-1858

3

The east elevation (view from Fourth Street). Essentially this is the Old Courthouse today. The large smokestack was removed when the heating plant was modernized. Historic American Buildings Survey drawing by Frank Leslie, 1937. Courtesy Jefferson National Expansion Memorial

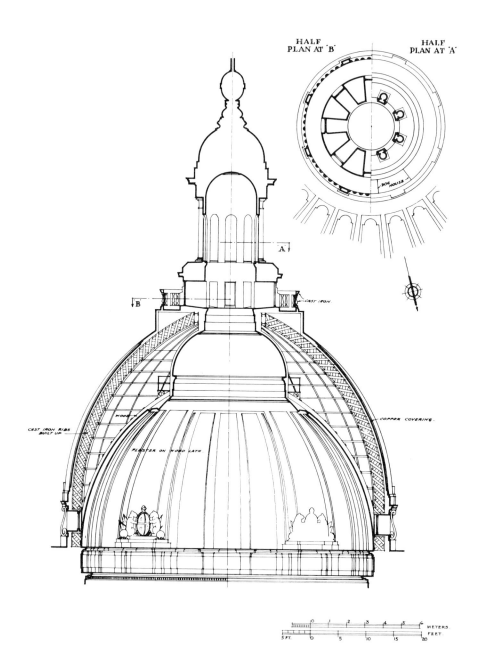

HALF
PLAN AT 'B'

HALF
PLAN AT 'A'

DOG HOUSE

A

B

CAST IRON

WOOD

CAST IRON RIBS
BUILT UP

COPPER COVERING.

PLASTER ON WOOD LATH

0   1   2   3   4   5   6   METERS

5 FT.   0   5   10   15   20   FEET

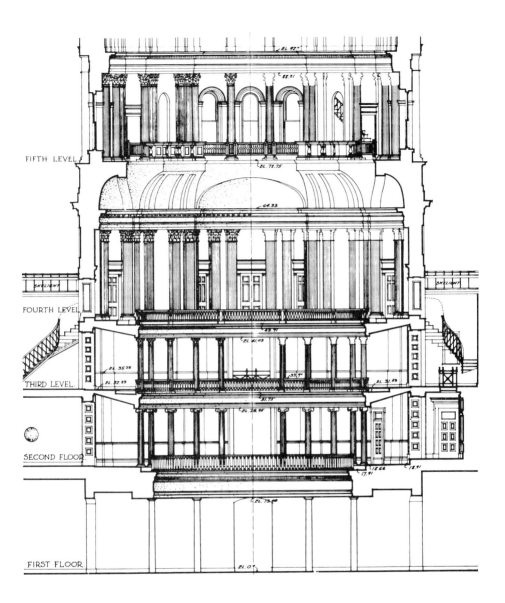

FIFTH LEVEL

FOURTH LEVEL

THIRD LEVEL

SECOND FLOOR

FIRST FLOOR

Opposite: *Section through Rumbold's innovative cast- and wrought-iron dome: note double layers.* HABS drawing by George Harkness III, 1934.

Above: *Section through rotunda, looking south.* HABS drawing by George Harkness III and Robert Price, 1934. Both Courtesy Jefferson National Expansion Memorial

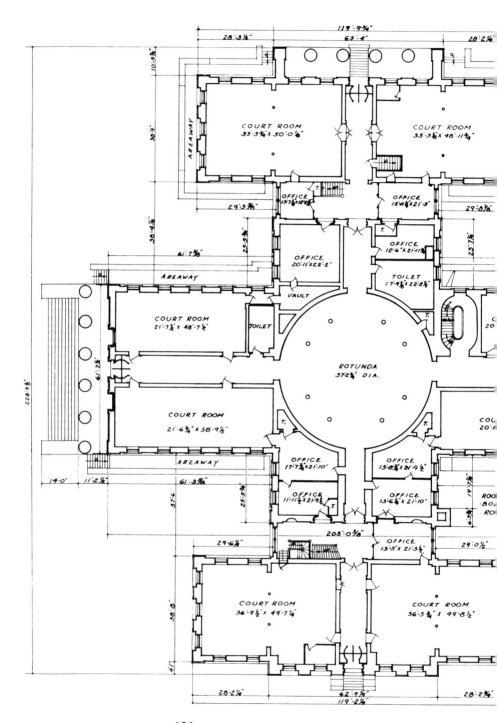

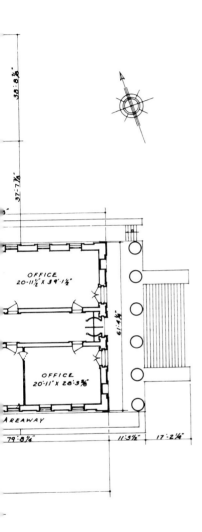

First Floor Plan as it was when last used for courts, 1930. Various of these spaces are now exhibition rooms and offices. HABS *drawing by Frank Leslie, 1937.* Courtesy Jefferson National Expansion Memorial

OFFICE
20·11½″ x 39′·1½″

OFFICE
20′·11″ x 26′·3⅝″

AREAWAY

79′·8¼″

11′·5½″   17′·2¼″

0 1 2 3 4 5 6 7 8 9 10 11 12 13 14 15 16 METERS

5ft. 0   5   10   15   20   25   30   35   40   45   50   FEET

127

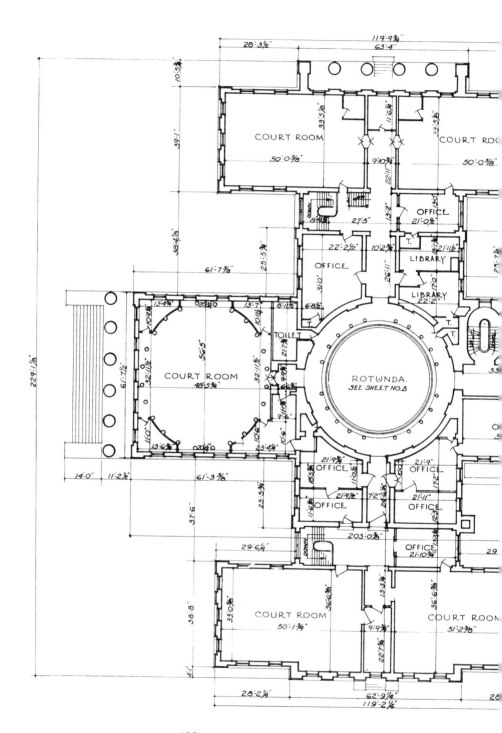

COURT ROOM
50'-0⅝"

COURT ROO(M)
50'-0⅝"

OFFICE
21'-0½"

T.

LIBRARY

OFFICE

LIBRARY
22'-2"

T.

T.
T.

TOILET

COURT ROOM
48'-5¾"
56'-5

ROTUNDA.
SEE SHEET NO.3

OFFICE
21'-9¾"

OFFICE
21'-9"

OFFICE

OFFICE
21'-11"

OFFICE
21'-10¾"

OFFICE
29

COURT ROOM
50'-1¾"

COURT ROOM
51'-2⅞"

229-1⅛"

119-9¾"
63'-4"
28'-3½"

10'-5¾

39'-1

38'-4⅜"

61'-7⅞"

25'-5¾

33'-5⅝

11'-6¼"

33'-5⅝

13'-2

21'-11½

25'-7¼

14'-0" 11'-2½" 61'-3⅝"

6'-7½"

37'-6"

25'-5¾

29'-6¼"

38'-8"

33'-0⅝

36'-6⅜

36'-6⅜

28'-2¼"

62'-9¼"
119'-2¼"

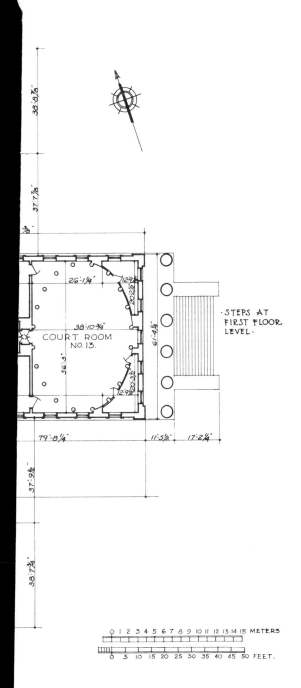

Second Floor Plan as it was when last used for courts, 1930. The two major courtrooms, in the east and west wings, have been restored: most of the other areas now are offices. HABS drawing by Frank Leslie and John Stephens, 1934. Courtesy Jefferson National Expansion Memorial

38'-8⅞"

37'-7⅞"

⅜"

26'-1¼"

12'-9½"

20'-2½"

·STEPS AT
FIRST FLOOR
LEVEL·

38'-10¾"

6'-4¼"

COURT ROOM
NO. 13.

56'-3"

20'-3½"

12'-9½"

79'-8¼"

11'-5½"

17'-2¼"

37'-9½"

38'-7¾"

0 1 2 3 4 5 6 7 8 9 10 11 12 13 14 15 METERS

0 5 10 15 20 25 30 35 40 45 50 FEET.